W9-BLT-847

A gift for:

....

From:

....

Date:

....

seeing *beautiful* again

50 DEVOTIONS
to find redemption in every part of your story

LYSA TERKEURST

THOMAS NELSON
Since 1798

Seeing Beautiful Again

Some material in this book has been previously published in *It's Not Supposed to Be This Way* and *Forgiving What You Can't Forget.*

Published in Nashville, Tennessee, by Thomas Nelson. Thomas Nelson is a registered trademark of HarperCollins Christian Publishing, Inc.

Thomas Nelson titles may be purchased in bulk for educational, business, fundraising, or sales promotional use. For information, please e-mail SpecialMarkets@ThomasNelson.com.

ISBN 978-1-4002-1891-2 (HC)
ISBN 978-1-4002-1888-2 (audiobook)
ISBN 978-1-4002-1893-6 (eBook)

Printed in China

21 22 23 24 25 GRI 10 9 8 7 6 5 4 3 2 1

To my sister, Angee.

The one who has known me the longest, who loves me the best, and who models this message of seeing beautiful again in extraordinary ways.

You were pure madness to me when you were born. I was dumbfounded that Mom thought having another baby was a good idea.

You were pure magic to me when I figured out you'd clean my room for a few pennies. I'm sorry for that and the mud pies.

You were pure mystery to me when I was a book nerd and you were the popular cheerleader.

You were pure bravery to me when you walked through your hardest season with courage, grace, and unwavering love for your amazing kids.

You were pure love to me when you walked me through my hardest season while holding my hand and my heart with fierce protection and absolute tenderness.

You are my person, my best friend, my (terrified of heights) adventure partner for life, and one of the best gifts God ever gave me. Angee, I love you forever, and I like you always.

Contents

1. The Process Before the Promise 13
2. The Best Place to Park Your Mind Today 17
3. I Don't Want This to Be a Part of My Story 22
4. Is This News or Truth? 27
5. When Joy Feels So Very Unrealistic 32
6. Why Would You Let This Happen, God? 36
7. Step After Step of Unwavering Obedience 40

A Letter from Lysa 44

8. Three Questions to Ask Before Giving a Response You Can't Take Back 45
9. Is It Really That Big of a Deal If I Stay Offended? 50
10. This Won't Be For Nothing 55
11. The Only Love That Never Fails 59
12. When I Deny Jesus 63

A Letter from Lysa 67

13. Three Perspectives to Remember When Your Normal Gets Hijacked 68
14. Saved by Suffering 72
15. Sometimes It's a One- or Two-Verse Day 77
16. When Things Get Worse Just Before They Get Better 81
17. The Blessings of Boundaries 87
18. Where Is My Happily Ever After? 91

A Letter from Lysa 95
19. When Giving Grace Feels Hard 96
20. Forgiveness: The Double-Edged Word 100
21. Please Don't Give Me a Christian Answer 105
22. When God Gives You More Than You Can Handle 110
23. An Unexpected Thread of Hope 114
24. A Script to Preach to Myself 119
A Letter from Lysa 123
25. Higher Perspective in Present Realities 124
26. A New Way to Walk and a New Way to See 128
27. When the Only Thing You Have Left to Give Is Time 133
A Letter from Lysa 138
28. God's Goodness Isn't Canceled 139
29. Why Isn't God Answering My Prayer? 144
30. When Our Opinions and Feelings Get Us in Trouble 149
31. The One We Really Need Today 154
A Letter from Lysa 158
32. When Unchangeable Feels Unforgivable 159
33. As Far As It Depends on Me 164
34. Suspicious of God 168
35. Brushstrokes of Compassion 172
A Letter from Lysa 177
36. About My Anger 178
37. The Daily Cure for a Heavy Heart 184
38. More Than Dust and Bone 189
39. When Your Husband Has Given Up 193

A Letter from Lysa 197

40. Five Things to Say to a Friend Today 200
41. Let Bitterness Be a Seed of Potential, Not a Root of Regret 205
42. Healing Is Such a Process 210

A Letter from Lysa 216

43. The Slippery Slope 217
44. You Are Worth Celebrating 222
45. The Verses I Need Today 226
46. The Best Thing You Can Do for Your Marriage Today 232

A Letter from Lysa 237

47. But How Do I Get Through the Next 86,400 Seconds? 238
48. I Still Get Scared Sometimes 242
49. Delicate, Not Fragile 247
50. Living Beautiful 251

Notes 257
A Prayer from Lysa 258
Beautiful Truths to Remember 260
About the Author 267
About Proverbs 31 Ministries 268
An Invitation from Lysa 269
Index by Topic 271
Index by Devotion 272

In the middle of the pain
you didn't cause,
the change you didn't want,
or the reality you didn't
know was coming . . .
your life can still be beautiful.

1

The Process Before the Promise

I waited patiently for the Lord; he
inclined to me and heard my cry.

Psalm 40:1 ESV

Are there any deep disappointments in your life that seem to be lingering on and on? Do you feel like you've prayed the same prayers over and over, with little to no change?

I understand how hard that is. Over the last few years, I've walked through some of the most heartbreaking seasons in my family, marriage, and health. And although the circumstances of your life may be different, you probably have your own middle-of-the-night moments wrestling through tears too.

There are memories that still hurt. Realities that make you wonder if you'll ever feel normal again. Sufferings that seem forever long. And you're disappointed that today you aren't living the promises of God you've begged to come to pass.

In your most private moments, you want to scream words you don't use around your Bible friends at the unfairness of it all. But then there are more hopeful moments . . . when you want to turn up the praise music, lift up honest prayers, and declare God is good even when the situation doesn't seem good.

Hurting but still hoping—that is the human journey.

And that is where we find David in Psalm 40. In the first ten verses, David praised God for delivering him, but then in verses 11 through 17, he was crying out for God to deliver him again. David was hurting but still hoping.

Hurting but still hoping—that is the human journey.

Hoping doesn't mean we ignore reality. No, hoping means we acknowledge reality in the very same breath that we acknowledge God's sovereignty—His absolute ability and power to work as He sees best.

Our hope can't be tied to whether or not a circumstance or another person changes. Our hope must be tied to the unchanging promises of God. We hope for the good we know God will ultimately bring from our situation, whether the good turns out to match our desires or not. And sometimes that takes a while. The process often requires us to be persevering and patient.

Honestly, I know that can feel a little overwhelming.

I want the promised blessing of Psalm 40:4: *"Blessed is the man who makes the Lord his trust"* (ESV), but I forget that this kind of trusting in God is often forged in the crucible of longsuffering. God isn't picking on me. God is picking me to personally live out one of His promises.

It's a high honor. But it doesn't always feel that way. I've got to walk through the low places of the process before I'm perfectly equipped to live the promise.

We read about some of the low places of the process in verses 1 through 3 of Psalm 40 (ESV):

I waited patiently for the LORD;
he inclined to me and heard my cry.
He drew me up from the pit of destruction,
out of the miry bog,
and set my feet upon a rock,
making my steps secure.
He put a new song in my mouth,
a song of praise to our God.
Many will see and fear,
and put their trust in the LORD.

The idea of waiting patiently in verse 1 is incredibly important in this psalm. The Hebrew word for *waiting* indicates it is ongoing, and it holds a sense of eager expectancy and hope.

So while I want the solid rock on which to stand, first I have to wait patiently for the Lord to lift me out of the slime and mud and set my feet. That word *set* in the original Hebrew is *qum*, which means to "arise or take a stand." God has to take me through the process of getting unstuck from what's been holding me captive before I can take a stand.

I also want that new song promised in the psalm. Did you notice, though, what comes before the promise of a new song? It's the many cries to the Lord for help. The most powerful praise songs are often guttural cries of pain that got turned into beautiful melodies.

I know this is hard. So, let me be the one to lean in and whisper these words to you as we begin to wrestle through this journey together: *"God is working things out. He's not far away. He is right here with us. We need to cling to this hope. Believe this hope. Live out this hope. Right here and right now. Even if our prayers aren't answered in the way and the timing we want. Even when this process feels messy. We will trust that God is good."*

Lord God, I know You often work in ways I don't understand. There are parts of my story that feel incredibly hard to live in, but I trust You are making something beautiful even out of those parts of my life. In Jesus' name, amen.

2

The Best Place to Park Your Mind Today

Finally, brothers and sisters, whatever is true, whatever is noble, whatever is right, whatever is pure, whatever is lovely, whatever is admirable—if anything is excellent or praiseworthy—think about such things.

Philippians 4:8

Before I even have my first cup of coffee most mornings, the mental battle begins. Lies bombard me with scripts that don't line up with the truth of God's Word and drag my mood down before I'm even given a fair shot to enjoy this new day.

The mess that was left in my kitchen the night before will turn into an entire mental dialogue about how disrespected I am and how inconsiderate and uncaring my people are. The truth is my people care deeply about me, but they are sometimes forgetful when they're up playing family games or having late-night chats. I wish my first inclination wasn't to personalize those dirty dishes, but the lies are loud and so convincing sometimes. I'll make a snarky comment out of frustration, which just sets the completely opposite tone in my home than what I really want. Then the guilt of my morning annoyance turns into lies about myself because I should be more patient and understanding.

And it's not just in my kitchen. The more I entertain the lies, the heavier my heart feels all day long. It's no longer just about the dishes and the comments I made that morning. Those lies quickly tap into the deeper wounds of my heart and deeper insecurities I have as a wife and a mother. Without even realizing it, those lies begin to inform my beliefs and steal my peace. The danger is that lies don't just pass through our thoughts. Lies ravage our beliefs.

Lies, unattended to, affect the perceptions we form. The perceptions we form eventually become the beliefs we carry. The beliefs we carry determine what we see. That's why we must be so careful to recognize where lies are affecting us. Our faith can get fractured by the lies we let inform our beliefs.

Our faith in God can get fractured by the lies we let inform our beliefs.

I've come to realize that what makes faith fall apart isn't doubt. It's being too certain of the wrong things.

The wrong things I'm tempted to believe can be:

- *It will never get better.*
- *My life will never be good again.*
- *God won't forgive me.*
- *I can't forgive them.*
- *I won't be able to get over this.*
- *God doesn't care.*

Instead of letting those defeating lies take over my emotions and dictate my reactions, I've learned to see them as warning signals. When I have a thought that is especially negative or condemning of myself or others, I pause to consider, "Is this really true?" And what I'm discovering is that most of the time the answer is, "No, it's not."

The Bible, while inspirational, is also very applicable. And when we turn to God's Word to know what to do with the thoughts and lies causing commotion in our minds, we can begin the work of transforming those first moments in the morning to holy moments. And then we can set a better pattern for all the other thoughts we have the rest of the day.

In the book of Philippians, we find Paul in prison writing to the church of Philippi. If there were ever a perfect situation for someone to start believing the wrong things about themselves, their people, and God, it's Paul writing a letter from prison. But he didn't waver. And in his closing words of Philippians 4, Paul addressed our thought-life as Christians:

> *Finally, brothers and sisters, whatever is true, whatever is noble, whatever is right, whatever is pure, whatever is lovely, whatever is admirable—if anything is excellent or praiseworthy—think about such things.* (v. 8)

Right. Pure. Lovely. Admirable. Praiseworthy. Those are the things to think about, and not just because they're a delightful and fun break from the lies we like to explore, but because they will bring you peace.

In the very next verse (9), Paul highlights this promise by emphasizing once more that when we put this instruction into practice the peace of God will be with us. I love that it doesn't say that the peace is dependent on our circumstances getting better. No, only that if we bring better thoughts to our circumstances we will have access to the best peace there is.

The peace of God. That is what I really long for.

Friend, rather than giving space to any lies that are trying to come in and set up camp in your mind today, remember that God has given instructions for a better place to park our thoughts. This doesn't mean we deny ourselves processing hard things or complicated relational struggles, but it does mean we intentionally direct our thoughts toward what is right, pure, lovely, admirable, and praiseworthy. In the midst of the messes, the frustrations, the aggravations, and irratations, I can still be a noticer of some good and redirect where I choose to park my mind. Is this self-help hype? No, it's the Truth that when applied, actually works. When we set our minds on the things of God, we will have direct and immediate access to the peace of God.

When we set our minds on the things of God, we will have direct and immediate access to the peace of God.

God, help me untangle any lie I'm believing and replace it with Your life-giving truth. Help me set my mind on things that are of You: Pure. Lovely. Admirable. Praiseworthy. In Jesus' name, amen.

3

I Don't Want This to Be A Part of My Story

He gives strength to the weary and
increases the power of the weak.

Isaiah 40:29

"Dear God, please don't let this be part of my story . . ."

I wrote this in my journal, unable to process how a God who loves me and promises to protect me could allow this diagnosis on top of an already devastating season.

When I first got my cancer diagnosis in the fall of 2017, my husband and I were separated. It wasn't my choice to live alone, and just about every single night during that intensely lonely season, I prayed with tears running down my face. I had been so sure God was going to move in a powerful way and somehow start making things turn around. But instead of things getting better, they just seemed to get worse and worse. And now cancer?

When life is unfolding in hard ways, it can feel impossible to understand why God would allow hurt upon hurt. How could His mercy not fix all of this? How could He possibly use any of this for good?

The biggest lesson I learned during that season is how limited our human vision really is. We see more and more unnecessary heartbreak. But God sees the exact pieces and parts that must be added right now to protect us, provide for us, and prepare us with more and more of His strength working through us.

We can't always assume the broken pieces of our life circumstances are terrible and pointless—not with our God.

We can't always assume the broken pieces of our life circumstances are terrible and pointless—not with our God.

One day as I was reading Genesis chapter 2, I realized that out of all the ingredients in the world, God chose dust to breathe life into and create mankind. Immediately I wrote in my journal how much this encouraged my heart and helped me realize something different about the circumstances of my life that seemed beyond repair and reduced to dust. I wrote, "Dust doesn't signify an end. It's often what must be present for new to begin."

A few days later I shared with a friend about how when we place the dust of our life into God's hands, and He mixes it with

His living water, the clay that's formed can then be made into anything. She smiled so big because her mom is a professional potter. She'd seen clay being formed into many beautiful things when placed into her mother's hands. And she shared something with me that made my jaw drop.

She told me that wise potters not only know how to form beautiful things from clay, but they also know how important it is to add some of the dust from previously broken pieces of pottery to the new clay. This type of dust is called "grog."

A good potter takes broken pieces of pottery and shatters them to make the grog most useful for adding it to new clay. When shattered just right, the grog dust added to the new clay will enable the potter to form that clay mixture into a larger and stronger vessel than it could otherwise be. And it can go through fires much hotter as well. Plus, when glazed, these pieces end up having a much more beautiful, artistic look to them than they would have otherwise.

Isn't that incredible?

And then I read Isaiah 45:9: *"Woe to those who quarrel with their Maker, those who are nothing but potsherds among the potsherds on the ground. Does the clay say to the potter, 'What are you making?' Does your work say, 'The potter has no hands'?"*

I kept reading that verse from Isaiah and decided to dive a little deeper into the term *potsherd*.

A potsherd is a broken piece of pottery. A broken potsherd can lie on the ground and be nothing more than a constant reminder of brokenness. It can also be used to continue to scrape us and hurt us even more when we grasp it in our hands. Or the Master Potter can be entrusted to take that potsherd, shatter it just right, and then use it in remolding us to make us stronger and even more beautiful.

When I understood this, I saw that God was keeping me moldable while adding even more strength and beauty in the process. Much like He promises in our key verse for today, *"He gives strength to the weary and increases the power of the weak"* (Isaiah 40:29).

I didn't want to have cancer.

There's no part of my human brain that thinks cancer is fair for any precious person who receives this diagnosis. God didn't cause this potsherd reality in my life. It's the result of living in this sin-soaked world.

But I had to decide I didn't want that broken reality to just be a potsherd wasted on the ground or something I kept in my hand that hurt me more. I had to take it and entrust it to the Lord.

He gives strength to the weary and increases the power of the weak (Isaiah 40:29).

What do you need to entrust to Him today?

God is making something beautiful out of our lives, sweet

friend. I truly believe it. We can keep questioning what He sees as the necessary ingredients to strengthen us, or we can choose to believe He can do amazing things with the dust and potsherds of our lives. I know it's not easy. But let's surrender every broken piece into the Father's hands.

Lord, I believe You see things I cannot see, so give me the courage to press in even when I'm resistant to what You are doing in my life. I know You have eventual good in mind, and I trust You with all my heart. In Jesus' name, amen.

4

Is This News or Truth?

Jesus answered, "I am the way and the truth and the life. No one comes to the Father except through me."

John 14:6

News and truth aren't always one and the same.

In the previous devotion, I told you about my breast cancer diagnosis in 2017 in one of the hardest seasons of my life. I wish I could properly describe what happened in the moment my doctor said: "Lysa, I'm so sorry. You have cancer."

Everything around me got incredibly quiet and seemed to move very slowly. I could hear the doctor continuing to talk, but I couldn't make out his words. I could feel words trying to form in my mouth, but there was no energy to actually speak. I knew I should probably cry, but no tears seemed available.

I am absolutely a woman who believes with all my heart that the presence of God is in the midst of my life. But in that moment, He felt distant and mysterious. I just felt stunned. And then I felt okay. And then I felt stunned again. I wanted to hold it together. But then falling apart seemed quite reasonable.

It's scary when doctors shock you with test results, and you don't know what the future holds.

But I will say during that time, God had so many people share simple words that became powerful revelations reminding me how very near God was to me. I think times of desperation often lead us to great revelations if we will make the choice to look for and be open to them each day.

One of those examples is an email I got from my friend Shaunti Feldhan. Her note said "Lysa, this is news. This is not truth."

Wow.

I've always thought of news and truth as one and the same. What the doctor gave me was news. Honest news, based on test results and medical facts.

But I have access to a truth that transcends news. The restoration that is impossible with human limitations is always possible for a limitless God. Truth factors God into the equation.

I have access to a truth that transcends news.

So I find myself looking at the word *impossible* a little differently today.

"Impossible," in light of Shaunti's note, could be completely different if I just stick an apostrophe between the first two letters. Then it becomes *I'm Possible*. God is the Great I AM. Therefore, He is my possibility for hope and healing.

I'm Possible is a much more comforting way to look at anything that feels quite impossible.

I suspect many of us have things in our life that feel impossible. Maybe you just got some bad news. News of an impossible financial situation. News of an impossible marriage situation. News of an impossible job situation. News of an impossible kid situation. News of an impossible friend situation. News of an impossible medical situation. News of an impossible current event situation.

Whatever news you just got or will get, I pray Shaunti's advice helps you too. What you heard is news, and this is God's truth:

"I AM MAKING A WAY"
"I am the way and the truth and the life. No one comes to the Father except through me." (John 14:6)

"I AM FOREVER FAITHFUL."
He is the Maker of heaven and earth, the sea, and everything in them—he remains faithful forever. (Psalm 146:6)

"I AM WITH YOU."
"So do not fear, for I am with you; do not be dismayed, for I am your God. I will strengthen you and help you; I will uphold you with my righteous right hand." (Isaiah 41:10)

"I AM HOLDING YOU."
Yet I am always with you; you hold me by my right hand. (Psalm 73:23)

"I AM YOUR HIDING PLACE."
You are my hiding place; you will protect me from trouble and surround me with songs of deliverance. (Psalm 32:7)

One of the greatest comforts to me through all this has been knowing that, somehow, God will use this for good. And that God will be my "possible" in the midst of what can sometimes feel so impossible.

Of course, I still have those less spiritually secure moments when I feel like I'm sinking into a consuming fear of the unknown.

But how thankful I am for the Great I AM. The One who will absolutely *"guide me in [His] truth and teach me"* (Psalm 25:5).

God will be my "possible" in the midst of what can sometimes feel so impossible.

I'm so sorry for whatever it is you're going through today that's making the tears flow and your heart sink. I'm praying for you today, my friend. I'm praying that every time the word *impossible* creeps up and starts to steal your hope, you will see the words *I'm Possible* and hold on to Him. He will help you through any news you get and remind you of what's ultimately true.

God, You are I AM, I'm Possible. You are the Way, the Truth, and the Life, and You are forever faithful. Help me lean on these truths when the news I receive feels impossible. In my home, in my family, and in my circumstances, I trust You. In Jesus' name, amen.

5

WHEN JOY FEELS SO VERY UNREALISTIC

Consider it pure joy, my brothers and sisters, whenever you face trials of many kinds, because you know that the testing of your faith produces perseverance.

James 1:2–3

There's no part of me that wants sorrow to be a part of my story. There isn't any plan God could present where I would willingly agree to heartbreak and pain.

But the longer I walk with God, the more I see what a tragedy that would be. Picking and choosing what gets to be part of my story would keep me from the ultimate good God has in mind.

If that seems hard to fathom in the midst of your own difficult circumstance today, I want to share some verses found in James that have helped me in my hardest seasons. I have to warn you, it might not feel good at first glance. But as we dig in together, I think you'll see it's better to wrestle with truth than to stay stuck in turmoil.

James 1:2–4 reminds us, *"Consider it pure joy, my brothers and sisters, whenever you face trials of many kinds, because you know that the testing of your faith produces perseverance. Let perseverance finish its work so that you may be mature and complete, not lacking anything."*

I confess I like these verses. Until I don't. These words are easy to pull out when your worst issue is that the drive-through coffee joint got your order wrong. They frappéed your latte and waylaid the start of your workday.

But what about those other things we walk through? The ones that hurt too long? Or disappoint too deeply? Or feel devastatingly permanent?

To slap some "we should be joyful about this" verses on top of the hard things feels cruel. Like a bad joke about something excruciatingly painful. It's just too soon for that kind of nonsense.

That's why I'm glad these verses don't say "feel the joy" but instead "consider where some glimpses of joy might be even in the midst of all the hurt."

Our understanding of joy rises and falls on whether we truly trust God in the middle of what our human minds can't see as good at all. It's hard. So I like to think of it in terms of baking. Imagine if we decided to make a cake from scratch today.

After going to the store, we set out all the ingredients: the flour, the butter, the sugar, the vanilla, the eggs, the baking powder, and a pinch of salt. But then maybe we felt too tired to mix it all together and make the cake. Instead, we thought we could just enjoy the cake one ingredient at a time. The thing is that sometimes we don't like some of the individual ingredients, so we'd rather leave them out.

The flour is too dry—leave it out. The sugar, butter, and vanilla are all good—leave them in! The eggs are just gross when raw—definitely leave those out! And then our cake would never be made "mature and complete, not lacking anything."

We are so quick to judge the quality of our lives and the reliability of God based on individual events, rather than on the eventual good God is working together.

We must know that just like the master baker has reasons to allow the flour and eggs in right measure into the recipe, Jesus, the author and perfecter of our faith (Hebrews 12:2 NASB), will do the same with dry times and hard times. And yes, we may have to go through some chaos in the mixing and some heat in the baking, but soon we will rise and live lives that are a sweet offering of hope, grace, peace, and comfort to others.

Sorrow and celebration can coexist together in a heart quite authentically. Mixing them together is part of the recipe of life.

That's how we can consider it pure joy today.

We can also make peace with the

fact that sorrow and celebration can coexist together in a heart quite authentically. Mixing them together is part of the recipe of life.

We can sit with and tend to all that still needs to be healed and at the same time laugh, plan for great things ahead, and declare this a glorious day.

To have both sorrow and celebration in our heart isn't denial.

It's deeming life a gift—even if it looks nothing like we thought it would right now.

Our sorrows make our hearts more tender and allow us to grieve. Our celebrations tend to our heart's need to recognize what is beautiful about our life, get back up, and go on.

Let's embrace the mix of all that's worthy of celebration while fully allowing sorrow to add what it brings as well—knowing we can trust Jesus' recipe of purpose in both the pain and joy.

Father God, when joy feels so very unrealistic, help me consider where glimpses of joy might be found throughout my day today. Help me bring the perspective of both "sorrow" and "celebration" to my circumstances and keep reminding me that Your plans for me are still good. In Jesus' name, amen.

6

Why Would You Let This Happen, God?

Elijah was afraid and ran for his life.

1 Kings 19:3

I have a really bad tendency when something hard or threatening happens. In a split second, all of the worst case scenarios pop into my mind and before I know it, my emotions start spiraling. I'm not sure why I have this tendency but the only way I've found to manage it is to pre-decide what truths I must factor into every event where I start to feel myself getting swept away in fear. These are three truths I literally speak out loud over and over:

1. God is good.
2. God is good to me.
3. God is good at being God.

This should be my starting place when looking at my circumstances. I'm not saying this is easy. But, these truths help me consider good things God might be doing, even with realities that don't feel at all good. They bring me back to the goodness of

God as the starting place for my continued trust in Him. When I don't do this on the front end of processing what's in front of me, I'll quickly start asking "Why would you let this happen, God?!"

I've had some really heartbreaking things happen in my life over the past couple of years. I had so many ideas of how my life should go, including notions of what a good God would and would not allow into my life.

I said I trusted God, but in reality, I think I trusted in the plan I *thought* God should follow. And when my life took shocking turns so far from my expectations, my soul shook. My peace evaporated. And everything in me wanted to run and hide and stop trusting God.

That is the exact place we find Elijah in 1 Kings 19. But to set up the context for what is happening, read the previous chapter, 1 Kings 18. We see God use Elijah to prove to the nation of Israel that He's the one true God in a miraculous and powerful way. Elijah must have been on a high, seeing God do what he expected God to do. And in essence, Elijah looked good himself as the "prophet who won the showdown at Mount Carmel."

But oh, how quickly things can change. How quickly Elijah's absolute trust in God evaporated with one death threat from Queen Jezebel. *"Elijah was afraid and ran for his life"* (1 Kings 19:3).

The events that took place in 1 Kings 18 and then 1 Kings 19 were both spectacular and sobering. Spectacular as we see the Lord magnificently prove His supremacy and might to all of

Israel. Sobering in that, in spite of God's tremendous showing of power, King Ahab and Queen Jezebel were not overthrown, and Elijah ended up running for his life into hiding.

Why was Elijah fearful and in despair? I have a feeling his desperation came from the same soul-shaking place I mentioned earlier—unmet expectations. Elijah probably assumed Ahab and Jezebel's unholy reign would come to an end after the mighty feat of the Lord. Yet that was not the outcome, and in that place of unfulfilled expectation, Elijah succumed to the fear of persecution.

Even though Elijah had experienced the miracle on Mount Carmel, he fled into the wilderness, exposing the truth that even a great prophet like Elijah was still human and could fall terribly short in terms of both faith and affection for the Lord.

Even so, the Lord dealt graciously and gently with Elijah—drawing him close with a whisper and giving him instructions for what to do next.

God didn't fix things the way Elijah thought they should be fixed, but He did lead him. And isn't it interesting the Lord led him back through the wilderness (1 Kings 19:15)? After all, that's often where God takes His people to teach them His perspective that blooms into deeper faith.

The Lord gave Elijah a second chance to face the same struggles he'd been dealing with before he ran and hid, except this time with right perspective and faith.

Elijah saw God's plan was good—even if it wasn't the way Elijah would have written it himself. And the same is true for us. God's plans don't have to match our plans for them to still be good.

What can we personally take away from studying these events in Elijah's life?

God's plans don't have to match our plans for them to still be good.

Perspective is the key to trusting God. And so often the clarity we need to see things from God's perspective comes from the wilderness experiences we all wish we could avoid.

Maybe the three truth filters that helped me can help you in whatever life circumstances seem unfair, unreasonable, or hurtful beyond what you can bear: God is good, God is good to me, God is good at being God.

Father God, I'm so thankful You don't condemn me for my fears. Help me use Your Word to preach truth to my own soul when I start to doubt Your goodness. Let it remind me that You see me, You love me, and I am safe—both in Your hands and in Your plans. In Jesus' name, amen.

7

Step After Step of Unwavering Obedience

"For my thoughts are not your thoughts, neither are your ways my ways," declares the Lord. "As the heavens are higher than the earth, so are my ways higher than your ways and my thoughts than your thoughts."

Isaiah 55:8–9

I am a planner. A problem-solver. So when I bring my struggles to the Lord in prayer, I tend to also bring my carefully thought-out ideas and suggestions He can choose from.

"Here's what I think will work, Lord. I just need You to sign off on one of these, okay?"

But the longer I walk with Him, the more I'm discovering that simply isn't the way God works. His ways? They aren't our ways (Isaiah 55:8–9).

In the previous devotion, we learned a valuable lesson from Elijah. Today I want to introduce you to another Old Testament friend who has something to teach us: Joshua.

In the sixth chapter of the book of Joshua, we find Joshua and the Israelites experiencing a problem of epic proportions. There was a massive wall preventing them from moving forward into their promised land.

I can't help but wonder what murmurs circled through the camp as they looked at the towering walls of Jericho. I'm sure there was no shortage of ideas or opinions on how they should tackle the wall.

But God didn't ask anyone for their opinion. *Not even Joshua.* Instead, He asked for their complete and unwavering obedience. Obedience in the face of a battle plan that would make no sense to their rational minds. A plan that actually involved no "battle" whatsoever.

All God wanted them to do was march. For six days straight, they were to march around the walls of Jericho. Then, on the seventh day of marching, they were to end with trumpet blasts and a great shout. God declared this mighty sound would bring the walls down.

What moves me most about the Israelites' part in this story isn't so much their willingness to take that first crazy step of obedience. It's how they *kept taking* steps of obedience. Step after step after step. Even though nothing appeared to change . . . even though there wasn't a single sign of cracking or crumbling in those massive walls . . . they kept marching.

What if they'd stopped after day two? Or day three? Or even day six?

Think of all they would have missed. They would have cheated themselves out of certain victory from God. And think of all the wasted and unnecessary energy, plus the risk of getting harmed, if they had attempted to tear down the wall themselves.

I don't say any of this casually—as if it's easy to keep going with God's instructions when there's no evidence of our situation changing. It's hard to continue marching when we don't see God move the way we thought He would. It's sometimes difficult to trust that He's working behind the scenes.

So what do we do when He asks us to move in ways that don't make sense to us? How do we keep "marching" when the situation still looks hopeless?

We make the same choice the Israelites made. We choose to walk by faith, not by sight (2 Corinthians 5:7). We take God at His word and hold fiercely to His promises (Hebrews 10:23).

It's hard to continue marching when we don't see God move the way we thought He would.

God had promised Joshua that He would deliver Jericho, its king, and its army into his hands (Joshua 6:2). And that is exactly what He did. When they marched around the city on that seventh day and gave their great shout with the blare of the trumpets, the walls fell down flat. Flat! The city was theirs for the taking (v. 20).

Their victory never hinged on their ability or any of their well-thought-out plans. It was solely dependent on their unwavering obedience offered to a loving and mighty God.

I don't know what steps of obedience God is currently calling you to take that don't make sense to you. But let me be the gentle whisper in your ear encouraging you to keep going. *Keep trusting. Keep taking step after step after obedient step.*

We don't have to understand the "why" of God's ways. But we do have to keep choosing to follow them.

Let's not stop short of our victory with God. He is working things out. He is present. His plan is still good, and He can still be trusted. These are certainties even when life feels so very uncertain.

Lord, I confess that at times my heart feels discouraged when I don't see immediate results from my steps of obedience. Thank You for reminding me that just because I can't see You moving, it doesn't mean You aren't. Please help me as I walk by faith not sight. Day after day. Step by step. In Jesus' name, amen.

A Letter from Lysa

Commit your way to the Lord; trust in him and he will do this.

Psalm 37:5–6

Beautiful friend, I don't know what your "this" is today, but I do know your best tactic isn't fighting back or fretting over the what-ifs or spending sleepless nights trying to figure it out.

Put on a worship song. Declare the name of Jesus over and over. Let Him fight for you.

Stare the feelings of doubt and defeat back to a shrunken-down place. Refuse the craving to numb out or lash out. And honor the Lord with your actions and reactions today.

The Devil wants you freaked out with fear. God wants you standing firm with faith. He will do this!

Keep marching,

Lysa

8

Three Questions to Ask Before Giving a Response You Can't Take Back

A gentle answer turns away wrath, but
a harsh word stirs up anger.

Proverbs 15:1

One day I was avoiding a conversation with someone who had already made it known to me that they didn't see things the way I did. I just knew it was going to be hard and probably not go well.

My heart raced when I saw their number pop up on my phone. Nothing in me wanted to have this conversation. I was beyond aggravated. Hurt. Angry. And tired of being misunderstood. Maybe you can relate.

I answered the call with two goals in mind: to prove how right I was and how wrong the other person was.

How do you think that conversation went?

Not well.

This conflict happened many years ago, so the rush of emotion has dissipated, and I can see more clearly how wrong my approach was.

And while I'm far from being in a place where I can shine my halo, I am getting better at not letting those initial thoughts of *I'll show you* leak into my reactions.

One thing that has helped me over the years has been memorizing—and making every effort to live out—our key verse for today, *"A gentle answer turns away wrath, but a harsh word stirs up anger"* (Proverbs 15:1).

When I dug into the deeper meaning of the word *gentle* in this verse I found that, in Hebrew, the word is *rak*. *Rak* is used sixteen times in Scripture and relates to the quality of being tender, soft, or delicate in substance. The connection with "answer" means our response should soothe and comfort the one listening to us.

This means that, as disciples of Jesus, we are called to exercise emotional restraint by giving soft responses rather than harsh or painful ones. This enables us to turn back wrath instead of stirring it up, which only serves to cause further damage.

So how do we walk this out practically? Even with—maybe especially with—people who have hurt us the most?

I have found it helpful to ask myself three questions.

1. What part of this issue can I own and apologize for?

Often when conflict occurs, two people have two opposing narratives about the situation at hand. And usually there isn't one person who is perfectly right or all-the-way wrong. I'm not talking about owning things that aren't ours to take on. But if there is a part that's mine, I don't want to let pride keep me from doing what's right.

If I make peace with the part I need to own and apologize for *before* the conversation, there's a greater chance I'll stay calm *in* the conversation, and it's the only way I've ever seen the other person's heart soften. But if I enter in with a heart set on retaliation, Proverbs 15:18 (ESV) reminds me it will result in conflict escalation: *"A hot-tempered man stirs up strife, but he who is slow to anger quiets contention."*

Usually, in conflict, there isn't one person who is perfectly right or all-the-way wrong.

2. HOW CAN I SOFTEN MY HEART TOWARD THIS PERSON SO I HONOR THEM DESPITE HOW THEY REACT?

This one is hard. Really hard. But I know hurt people hurt people.

Usually the person with whom I'm having a conflict has some kind of past or current hurt in their life feeding this issue. Chances are that hurt doesn't have anything to do with me, but it's adding to their emotional response in this conflict.

Softening my heart is easier if I can sympathize with the hurt I can't see. Again, if I can duck below my pride, honor will be my reward. Proverbs 29:23 reminds us, *"Pride brings a person low, but the lowly in spirit gain honor."*

3. If I knew this conversation was being recorded and then shared with people I greatly respect, how would this change my reaction?

What if I showed up to church this week, and my pastor directed everyone to watch the screen for an example of a bad reaction? And then my face appeared. Have. Mercy. I would surely faint.

While it is highly unlikely that our conversations will be recorded and viewed, it is very likely others are watching our reaction. Children. Coworkers. Friends. But here's the one that really grabs my attention—my Jesus is very much present. Philippians 4:5 reminds us, *"Let your gentleness be evident to all. The Lord is near."*

Every conflict has variables to consider. Some conflicts have escalated to the point where professionals must be asked to help. Be mindful and prayerful about when this becomes a needed and wise step to take.

But for the everyday conflicts we all have, these questions are good to consider. And our key verse from today, Proverbs 15:1, is such a good reminder that reactions matter. If we control our reactions in the short term, we won't have to live with "reaction regret" in the long term!

My job is to be obedient to God. God's job is everything else. This measure of surrender is just another way we open our arms wide to the beauty God wants to create through us.

Dear Lord, please help me pause and allow the Holy Spirit to intervene when I want to react in ways that don't glorify You. Even when I'm caught off guard, may Your love and patience be the spillover from my heart. In Jesus' name, amen.

9

Is It really that big of a deal if I stay offended?

Joseph went after his brothers and found them near Dothan. But they saw him in the distance, and before he reached them, they plotted to kill him.

Genesis 37:17–18

Today there will be a moment. No one will snap a picture of it. It probably won't make it into the pages of those who journal. Or linger in the thoughts we carry with us to sleep tonight.

It will come.

It will go.

It will slip by seemingly unnoticed. But its effects won't slip. They'll stay. And if fostered, they will grow to epic proportions.

This is the moment when something creeps into our heart and pulls our focus from *right* to *wrong*. It will be just a hint of distortion. The smallest amount. But a slight and seemingly insignificant amount of skewed thought will take root.

And grow beyond what we can even imagine.

Which brings us to one of my favorite stories in the Bible. The one where Moses goes to Pharaoh and sings that song, "Oh, Pharaoh, Pharaoh, whoa, whoa, gotta let my people go."

Totally a loose translation, but if you've ever attended Vacation Bible School as a child, you probably know what I'm talking about.

There's an astounding chain of events that led up to God having to deliver His people from Pharaoh's fierce grip that I want us to trace and consider. It starts with this question: Why was the *entire* nation of Israelites—all God's people—all twelve tribes—enslaved in Egypt?

As I trace this story backward, I find it's because of one seemingly insignificant moment.

The course of history was changed because some siblings got offended and allowed that offense to grow into bitterness toward their brother Joseph. Envy and anger slipped in, which gave way to hatred; and eventually a full-force murderous fury propelled them to do the unthinkable.

There's never just a little bit of bitterness, a little bit of hatred, a little bit of holding onto an offense. Especially when we find ourselves already feeling vulnerable in a really hard season.

Our key verses, Genesis 37:17–18, reveal the moment the seeds of jealousy and offense bloomed into hatred and eventually into a full-blown plan to kill their brother, Joseph.

Joseph was thrown in a pit, and instead of killing him they decided to sell him as a slave.

After years of heartbreak and confusion passed, Joseph stayed close to God even though life was hard. And God's favor was on him.

Joseph continued through a long journey of many ups and downs, and eventually he unexpectedly landed in a position of great power in Egypt. Because of his position, when a famine hit the land, Joseph was in charge of the food supply. Later, the famine caused the brothers to travel to Egypt looking for food. Joseph had a choice to make: to force the brothers to pay for what they had done to him or forgive them. He chose forgiveness. And later, all eleven brothers and their families moved to Egypt. Joseph and his brothers make up what became the twelve tribes of Israel. As these tribes multiplied, they became the nation of Israel.

What the brothers meant for evil, God used for good. He saved the Israelites from the famine. But there were still lasting effects of the brothers' choices that played out years later.

After Joseph died, *"a new king, to whom Joseph meant nothing, came to power in Egypt. 'Look,' he said to his people, 'the Israelites have become far too numerous for us. Come, we must deal shrewdly with them or they will become even more numerous and, if war breaks out, will join our enemies, fight against us and leave the country.' So they put slave masters over them to oppress them with forced labor, and they built Pithom and Rameses as store cities for Pharaoh"* (Exodus 1:8–11).

So the entire nation of Israel suffered oppression and slavery for centuries. Why? Because a few brothers on an ordinary day got offended and jealous and allowed anger and revenge to slip in. And the moment these emotions were allowed to run rampant, the course of history changed.

In a moment.

May we never assume our moments don't matter. The decisions we make every second of every day matter. There are no little moments or little sins. There's a domino effect to it all.

So I fall hard upon soft grace. I thank God for this realization. I ask Him to make my soul even more sensitive, more aware, more in tune to my constant need for forgiveness.

There are no little moments or little sins. There's a domino effect to it all.

Though I'm weak, I walk in the strength of utter dependence. And I refuse to beat myself up for mistakes made yesterday. Today is a new day. A new chance to set things going in a different direction.

Joseph's brothers had years to try and rescue Joseph, find out where he was, help him, and set their past mistakes right. Years. They had years. But they never did set out to turn things around.

Oh, dear friend, we can't let today slip by. Moments matter.

Let's watch for any moment today when we have the choice

to let anger, envy, or something else negative get into our hearts and dictate how we act and react. Let's be aware of our feelings so they can drive us toward God, not into the enemy's traps. Our feelings are indicators there's a problem to attend to, but they should never dictate how we act and react.

Dear Lord, You made me. You know me. I need Your help where I am weak. Help me see today that even the smallest moments really do matter. Make me aware of any place where I'm off course in any area of my life, and give me the courage and the grace to do what pleases You. I want to do Your will. In Jesus' name, amen.

10

This Won't Be For Nothing

You intended to harm me, but God intended it for good to accomplish what is now being done, the saving of many lives.

Genesis 50:20

Do you ever worry that all your hard times and suffering will be for nothing? That all this pain you keep trying to press through is completely and utterly pointless?

I deeply understand that kind of fear and fatigue. When you pray the same prayers over and over, with little to no change, disappointments can turn into disillusionments.

That's why I wish I could give you a gift today. It's actually one I received myself in the middle of the most heartbreaking season of my marriage.

When my husband, Art, and I realized our marriage wasn't going to make any progress without some professional help, we started seeing an amazing counselor. We spent more than seventy-five hours in his office. It was all with the understanding that Art and I were on the same page, moving ahead *together.* All the devastation would be repaired, restored, and made right.

But during one of our sessions, my counselor discerned that we'd leave his office and walk into one of the fiercest seasons of this battle. He took a professionally mounted frame off his office wall and tore the backing to open it. He pulled out a real Purple Heart, the high honor the government gave his family when his brother-in-law was killed in the line of duty trying to save others.

Then he knelt in front of us and placed this priceless medal in my hand.

"Hold on to this, Lysa, for as long as you need it. When the battle gets so fierce you wonder if you will survive, remember this moment of me telling you that you will make it through this. If God gave out Purple Hearts, you would absolutely receive this high honor. What you are going through won't be for nothing. Your hurt will not be wasted. It will be for the saving of many lives."

Your hurt will not be wasted.

Speechless, I looked down at this beautifully outrageous gift. The moment stole all my words, and I had nothing to offer back to him but tears. I mouthed the words, "Thank you." I felt brave that day.

Less than a month after we returned home from that counseling appointment, my heart was devastated again.

I couldn't breathe. The medal was the only physical thing I felt I could hold, when every bit of my life was flying around as shattered debris. I thought we were almost done with that horrific season, and then I realized we hadn't even started the healing.

And while that Purple Heart couldn't heal me, it sure steadied me for the next couple of years, as Art and I did the hard work to put our marriage back together again.

I want to be that friend who helps steady you today, dear friend. Because I know what it's like to feel battle-weary.

As we talked about in a previous devotion, Joseph, who spoke the words in today's key verse, was familiar with feelings of discouragement and fatigue due to the betrayal of his brothers. How could you be thrown into a pit by your family, sold into slavery, and then unfairly imprisoned . . . without wondering if any good could ever come of your story?

But God had a plan. And the brothers' betrayal was not the end of Joseph's story. From pit to palace, Joseph was positioned to spare not only the lives of his family but the entire nation of Israel. This is why his words to his brothers in Genesis 50:20 are such a beautiful picture of redemption and hope: *"You intended to harm me, but God intended it for good to accomplish what is now being done, the saving of many lives."*

God has a plan for your life too. The enemy is going to try to trip you and rip you to shreds with the hurtful hisses that all of this suffering is for nothing. Don't you dare listen. God can still bring good from what feels impossible. You will see beautiful even from what feels too far gone.

You will see beautiful even from what feels too far gone.

I'm holding a Purple Heart in my hand that reminds me how so much of what we go through isn't just for us—it's for the saving of others. This message calling forth bravery in my soul isn't just for me. It's for you too. I knew the minute the counselor put it in my hand, it should be pinned on your chest as well. And if you were here with me today, I'd do just that. I would remind you that your story, surrendered into the hands of God, will not be wasted.

Close your eyes and breathe. You're brave, beautiful, and handpicked. A decorated soldier in this real battle with a glorious ending. I'm declaring over you that the Lord will restore you, redeem you, and write His glorious story onto the pages of your life.

Lord, I'm so thankful to know there isn't a single thing the enemy can send my way that You can't overcome, redeem, and use for my good and others' good. I'm choosing to surrender every heartache and difficult circumstance into Your hands today. In Jesus' name, amen.

11

The Only Love That Never Fails

The LORD your God is in your midst, a mighty one who will save; he will rejoice over you with gladness; he will quiet you by his love; he will exult over you with loud singing.

Zephaniah 3:17 ESV

If you've ever heard me give my testimony, you know part of what I share is being a little girl twirling around next to my biological daddy, wishing I could know he loved me.

Maybe in his own way he did. But something was broken in our relationship that left me feeling desperate for reassurance. Especially when he packed up all his things and left our family for good.

It's hard when the ones who are supposed to love us and lead us well, don't.

Maybe that statement rings painfully true for you. As we open up Zephaniah 3 together today, we will see it was a reality for the children of Israel too.

Zephaniah 3:3–4 vividly portrays the type of leadership the Israelites were under: *"Her officials within her are roaring lions;*

her judges are evening wolves that leave nothing till the morning. Her prophets are fickle, treacherous men; her priests profane what is holy; they do violence to the law" (ESV).

I can't help but read these words and think about how easy it would have been for God's people to point their fingers and attribute their sinful ways to the ones who led them.

But instead of fixing their eyes on the faults of their leaders, God invited them to redirect their focus to the goodness found in Him. He alone is righteous. He alone does no wrong (v. 5).

And instead of casting blame, God instructed them to own their sin and call upon His name (v. 9). He alone had the power to heal their hearts and remove their shame.

The prophet Zephaniah went on to reveal why the Israelites could feel safe placing all their trust in the Lord: "*The Lord your God is in your midst, a mighty one who will save; he will rejoice over you with gladness; he will quiet you by his love; he will exult over you with loud singing*" (v. 17 ESV).

This description of their God and King points back to one of Israel's first kings, David, who was both a warrior and a musician. It also paints an incredible picture of hope. One of a heavenly Father who not only loves His people and saves them but also sings over them with joy.

This may be an image we struggle to connect with in our own lives, though. Especially if our experiences with earthly leadership have left us feeling unloved, unprotected, and uncertain to the point we don't want to risk trusting anyone again. All too often, our view of God is tainted by the people who have failed us.

And it can be so tempting to point to hurts from our past and say, "All my issues can be linked back to what other people did to me."

Trust me. I know.

It's been more than twenty-five years since I've seen my dad—by his choice. That's hard on a girl's heart. But God doesn't want us to stay stuck in our places of blame and hurt. He wants to heal us and help us move forward.

Where my dad fell so short, God has filled in the gaps. Through His promises, I've been reassured of all those things I wished my earthly father would have said. I have learned that God's love for me is deep, unwavering, and certain.

I don't know what from your past still causes you pain today, friend. Perhaps you feel defeated and discouraged. Head down in shame. Hands hanging limp like the children of Israel. Or maybe what you faced has left your heart raging. Fists balled tight. Chin lifted in defiance. A heart ready to battle anyone who might try to hurt you again.

But I do know that the only thing that will stop the desperation, the uncertainties, the insecurities, is to realize those people who unfairly rejected us were putting their own hurt on display much more than making a defining statement about you. I want you to remember that just because they projected hurt on you doesn't mean you have to carry it the rest of your life or let it define you in any way. What they did doesn't mean you only deserve scraps of love from others. You are fully known and fully loved by a God whose greatest joy is to be with you.

You are fully known and fully loved by a God whose greatest joy is to be with you.

I pray these truths flood your heart with peace like they do mine. Peace that gives you permission to live like you are loved.

Because you are.

Deeply. Abundantly. And with a love that will not fail.

God, thank You for being a God who fights for me and takes delight in me. Even when I feel rejected and abandoned by those who have not loved me well, give me the ears to hear the song of love You're singing over my heart and life today. Thank You for your perfect, never-failing love. In Jesus' name, amen.

12

When I Deny Jesus

Immediately the rooster crowed the second time. Then Peter remembered the word Jesus had spoken to him: "Before the rooster crows twice you will disown me three times." And he broke down and wept.

Mark 14:72

"God, give me relief from my unbelief." I pray this not because I don't believe God is real and that God is good. I pray this when what He allows into my life does not feel good or seem good to me. When we assume we know what a good God would do, and He doesn't do it? That's when things can start to get a bit complicated. It's the place where doubts are formed and disappointment grows. The place where we can be tempted to distance ourselves from God with a heart of distrust.

I can't help but think about Peter—a man who boldly declared to Jesus, *"Even if I have to die with you, I will never disown you"* (Mark 14:31), but then found himself doing the exact opposite.

Let's take a closer look at Peter's story in Mark 14.

While we see Jesus remaining faithful in the midst of the pain and turmoil of a beloved friend's betrayal (vv. 43–45) and the high priest's interrogation (vv. 53–65), we find Peter with faltering faith as he stood waiting in a courtyard (vv. 66–72).

Afraid. Cold. Forgetful. Peter soon denied the One who loved him most.

Once. Twice. Three times. A rooster's shrill cry ushered in the shocking realization that the very thing Peter swore he'd never do, he did.

And as much as we might want to shake our head at Peter, I for one know I can't. Because I get it. I really do. I know what it's like to have intentions that are good but follow-through that falls to pieces. It's easy to say the words—we're all in for Jesus, and we'll do anything He asks of us. But then we get rejected or hurt by someone or become afraid we'll fail, and it becomes difficult to live out those words.

Fear, pain, and insecurities can really do a number on our hearts.

They certainly did a number on Peter's, as he watched Jesus, the One he had seen perform miracles, allow Himself to be bound and arrested. Jesus was supposed to be the King who would deliver the Jewish people from the oppression of the Romans. How could this be happening? Peter didn't realize this was the *only* way he or anyone else could experience Jesus reigning as King in eternity.

So, in a moment of doubt and disappointment, Peter chose to distance himself from Jesus. Distancing himself to the point of complete denial.

To deny something is to declare it's untrue. To deny *Jesus* is to say with our words, thoughts, or actions that we don't really believe the truth of who Jesus says He is or what He says He'll do.

How heartbreaking. For us. For Jesus.

But before we give in to feelings of shame, let's look at Luke 22:61–62. This passage gives us a slightly different glance at the moments immediately following Peter's final denial: *"The Lord turned and looked straight at Peter. Then Peter remembered the word the Lord had spoken to him: 'Before the rooster crows today, you will disown me three times.' And he went outside and wept bitterly."*

The look that passed between Jesus and Peter wasn't one of condemnation. It wasn't an "I told you so" moment. I believe Jesus' eyes were filled with compassion for Peter. The same compassion He has for us today. A look that invites us to trust Him and draw near to Him once again.

Oh, friend. We need to ask ourselves where we're denying Jesus' truth in our lives. Where are we denying Jesus' healing? Or denying Jesus' forgiveness—for ourselves or others? Where are we denying Jesus' redemption? Where are we denying Jesus' hope?

Nothing is beyond the reach of our Jesus. In Him, everything is certain. No matter what we've done. No matter what the enemy or our life's circumstances may say. *Nothing* is beyond the reach of Jesus. And I know today when we confess where we may be denying Him in our lives, He will look at us with the same compassion He did with Peter.

Nothing is beyond the reach of our Jesus.

So when doubts form and disappointments drag us down, we don't have to give in to the tempting voice of the enemy telling us to distrust God. We draw near to the Lord and pray, "I don't have to understand this to trust You with this. I will not deny Your power just because I'm afraid and I don't see evidence of You working now, God. I will kneel in prayer and ask You to help give me relief from any and all unbelief. And then I will rise up again and keep watching for evidence of all You are doing, big and small."

Dear Lord, please forgive me for ever doubting You. Forgive me for denying You. I turn my eyes to You and proclaim today that You are the Christ. The One my soul longs for. The One who suffered so I wouldn't have to. Give me relief from my unbelief. In Jesus' name, amen.

A Letter from Lysa

My dear friend,

If you're in a low valley right now, I know what that looks like—what that feels like. But let me speak life into your worn-out, broken-down, hurting heart just for a moment.

I've lived the horrors where I couldn't see any way out. But there's always a way with God. Stay close to Him. Stay close to people who love Him. Ask God to open the eyes of your heart so you can see circumstances through the lens of His truth. His perspective. His assurance. God will help you. Heal you. Somehow bring good from this and bring you through this.

He will make a miraculous way. One that you couldn't have imagined but one that is perfectly timed and planned.

I love you. I'm praying for you.

Lysa

13

Three Perspectives to Remember When Your Normal Gets Hijacked

"Abba, Father," he said, "everything is possible for you. Take this cup from me. Yet not what I will, but what you will."

Mark 14:36

The only way I could fall asleep was to lie to myself. *If you can just fall asleep, when you wake up you'll realize this is a nightmare that will soon end.*

But that wasn't reality. The next morning I woke up, and the devastation was there in an even more heartbreaking way. I reached across the covers and all my fears were confirmed.

My husband was gone.

Death hadn't taken him. No, the hijacking of our normal was a slow erosion that led to an eventual landslide, wiping out everything secure about our relationship.

That awful morning happened a few years ago. And I promised myself if I actually survived looking my greatest fears in the face, I would eventually be a voice of help and hope for others thrust into a darkness they never imagined.

So here I am. I survived. We survived. And we're determined to turn our battle scars into a battle cry to help others.

Whether you're reeling from a life-altering circumstance or you're wrestling through something not turning out the way you thought it would, I know what it's like to say, "It's not supposed to be this way." And I feel compelled to tell you three truths you must hear.

1. You are not alone in wanting things to be different and asking God to change your situation.

Did you know even Jesus asked God to change His circumstances and fix what God surely could have fixed in an instant? Listen to these words of Jesus right before He was arrested and eventually crucified: "*'Abba, Father,' he said, 'everything is possible for you. Take this cup from me . . .'*" (Mark 14:36). I have found such comfort in remembering the humanity of Jesus. Yes, His divinity made Him perfect and sinless, but His humanity felt the brutal weight of human hurt. He understands loneliness, betrayal, and being devastated by people He should have been able to trust. He knows what it's like to be lied to, misunderstood, falsely accused, and rejected. And because I know He's felt what I feel, I know I can trust Him to lead me through my heartbreak.

2. There is a place to attach our hope, but it's not to our desire for changed circumstances.

Our key verse, Mark 14:36, doesn't end with Jesus' request for things to be different. It ends with the strongest statement of trusting God that I can find in the whole Bible: *"Yet not what I will, but what you will."*

In other words, Jesus had a strong desire for change. But He had an even stronger desire to trust God with it all. This is hard for a girl like me, who loves to suggest to God all the ways He could surely fix my circumstances. But God loves me too much to do things my way. His plan is always better, even if I can't understand or see it clearly as it's unfolding.

3. Though our stories take unexpected twists and turns through valleys, God's plan is still good.

Only God could take a string of really bad circumstances and add them together to make a good I never knew was possible. Through the journey Art and I went on, none of my suggestions to fix things worked. The good only came in God's timing and in unexpected ways. And through the process, we've gained a deeper awareness of who God is and a strength that comes with truly trusting Him. Don't give up, dear friend. Don't stop praying. Don't stop hoping and believing. But also, don't believe that your way of getting to the other side of your circumstance is the only way. God has a perfect plan for a path to a renewed joy and a redeemed future that's probably one you can't even fathom. Trust Him.

I no longer lie to myself. Now the only way I can fall asleep at night is to speak truth: God is here. God is near. God can absolutely be trusted with it all.

God is here.
God is near.
God can
absolutely be
trusted with it all.

Father God, devastating circumstances have left me so weary. When things in my life feel so uncertain, I am tempted to shrink back in fear. But when I press into the truth of Your love, it leaves me hopeful. Even when my normal gets hijacked, thank You for the promise that You are the same yesterday, today, and forever. In Jesus' name, amen.

14

Saved by Suffering

The Lord is near to all who call on him,
to all who call on him in truth.

Psalm 145:18

I woke up on what I thought would be an ordinary Monday a few summers ago, but nothing was normal. I felt as if knives were mercilessly carving their way through my insides. I had never been in this much physical pain before. Waves of nausea left me convulsing and desperate for relief. I tried to step out of bed, but I collapsed. I screamed.

My family rushed me to the emergency room where we all hoped I could find some relief and help. But as panic gave way to desperation, I cried out for God to help me: "Take the pain away! Please, dear God, take this pain away!"

But He didn't. Not that moment. Not the next. Not even the next day.

His silence stunned me. My trust in Him in those moments started to feel shaky.

I kept picturing Him standing beside my bed, seeing my

anguish, watching my body writhing in pain, hearing my cries, but making the choice to do nothing. And I couldn't reconcile that.

How could God do that? How could He say I'm His daughter whom He deeply loves but let me lie there in excruciating pain?

These are the thoughts and questions that tumbled around my brain during a time of such pain and distress. I think we have all asked questions like this.

Where are You, God?

Do You see me?

Do You care?

After five of the longest and most excruciating days of my life, a new doctor came to my hospital room. He ran one last test. And finally, we had some answers.

Where are You, God? Do You see me? Do You care?

The right side of my colon had torn away from the abdominal wall and twisted around the left side. The blood flow was completely cut off. My colon had distended from the normal four centimeters in diameter to more than fourteen centimeters.

It had been in danger of rupturing when it was around ten centimeters, at which point I would have felt relief from the intense pain. And it's at that exact time when many others suffering with this medical situation feel that relief and go to sleep. Their bodies turn septic, and they die.

The surgeon explained that he needed to rush me into emergency surgery, and he'd be removing most of my colon. He was hoping to save enough that my body would eventually function properly again, but he wasn't sure.

He wasn't even sure I'd make it through surgery.

And with that daunting news, I hugged my family, prayed with my pastor, and I was wheeled into the surgical unit. Thankfully, the surgery went well, and weeks later while I was home recovering, the surgeon called me. He'd gotten the report back from the mass that was removed, and there was no further treatment needed. However, there was an alarming part of the report he couldn't reconcile.

He said, "Lysa, I don't really like how people throw around the term *miracle*. But honestly, it's the only word I know to use in your case. The cells in your colon were already in a state of autolysis. This is where your brain has signaled your body to start the process of decomposition. It's what happens when you die. Lysa, you can't get any closer to death than that. How you survived this, I can't explain."

I hung up the phone, stunned.

And I suddenly thought of those days before the surgery when I was begging God to take away the pain. I had questioned God because of the pain. I had wondered how God could let me be in so much pain. And I had cried, because I thought God somehow didn't care about my pain.

But in the end, God used the pain to save my life. The pain was what kept me in the hospital. The pain was what kept me demanding the doctors run more tests. The pain was what made me allow a surgeon to cut my belly wide open. The pain was what helped save me. Had God taken away the pain, I would have gone home, my colon would have ruptured, my body would have turned septic, and I would have died.

I now have a completely different picture of God standing beside my hospital bed while I was hurting and begging Him to help me. He wasn't ignoring me. No, I believe it took every bit of holy restraint within Him to *not* step in and remove my pain. He loved me too much to do the very thing I was begging Him to do.

He knew things I didn't know. He saw a bigger picture I couldn't see. His mercy was too great. His love was too deep. Indeed, He is a good, good Father.

He was not far off like I'd imagined as I lay writhing in pain. He was near. So very near. Just like Psalm 145:18 tells us, "*The LORD is near to all who call on him, to all who call on him in truth.*"

He was loving me through the pain. It was necessary pain—life-saving pain I can see now with new eyes. It's given me a whole new outlook on times when God seems silent.

God's silence was part of the rescue.

God's silence was part of the rescue. And I pray today that you would find rescue in even the excruciating moments when God feels silent. When you want to pull away, I pray today you have the courage to press in because you have a new perspective of God in the midst of your pain.

Father, You know the heartache and pain I am facing. Help me trust and believe You are not far off but are very close—holding me, comforting me, and not leaving me by myself to figure it all out. I know You are good, and You work all things together for my good—even my suffering. I absolutely trust You with every detail of my life. In Jesus' name, amen.

15

Sometimes It's a One- or Two-Verse Day

Pay attention to what I say; turn your ear to my words. Do not let them out of your sight, keep them within your heart; for they are life to those who find them and health to one's whole body.

Proverbs 4:20–22

Do you ever get overwhelmed when you sit down to read your Bible? There are so many books, deep thoughts, spiritual insights, and life-altering truths—where do we begin for today?

My sticky farm table and I have a long history of early mornings together. I gather up my Bible and my journal. I push past the sleepy feelings begging me to go back to my bed. And I look at the well-worn book as my love letter from God.

Truly, His words are a lifeline to me. A whisper from my God. A personal note. A treasure.

Of course, I don't always find myself in a season when I can consume chapters at a time. There have been days it has taken every ounce of energy in me to open my Bible and spend time with God. Not because I don't love Him. But because I felt spent. Worn down by the heaviness of my unchanging circumstances.

So on those days, quite honestly, it's just one or two verses that I tuck into my heart, so I can live out our key scripture: *"Pay attention to what I say; turn your ear to my words. Do not let them out of your sight, keep them within your heart; for they are life to those who find them and health to one's whole body"* (Proverbs 4:20–22).

This is what I want to do. I want to really pay attention. I need to listen well to what God is saying. I look for one verse I can savor word by word, letting it sink in deeply—interrupting me, rearranging me, redirecting me.

And I pray, "Dear God, what plans have I made for today that this verse needs to interrupt?

God, what thoughts did I bring in from yesterday that this verse needs to rearrange?

And God, what heart attitudes have I been carrying that this verse needs to redirect?"

His Word is the protective covering over my plans, my mind, and my heart. To let me run free without it will surely find me tripping over my own vulnerable insecurities and weaknesses. So with His love letter, He reminds me to pause.

- Pause and let the Holy Spirit intervene in my natural-flesh response with my people.

- Pause so I don't make the conversations all about me.
- Pause and remember I'm not always right.
- Pause to see the blessings, so many blessings, and say thank you at least once an hour.
- Pause to serve, pause to give, pause to encourage when everyone else rushes by.

The book of Proverbs has even more to say on how taking the time to cherish God's Word can lead to us being changed by His Word. For example:

> *My son, if you accept my words and store up my commands within you, turning your ear to wisdom and applying your heart to understanding—indeed, if you call out for insight and cry aloud for understanding . . . Then you will understand what is right and just and fair—every good path.* (2:1–3, 9)

> *Do not forsake wisdom, and she will protect you; love her, and she will watch over you. The beginning of wisdom is this: Get wisdom. Though it cost all you have, get understanding. Cherish her, and she will exalt you; embrace her, and she will honor you.* (4:6–8)

We don't have to get overwhelmed with the enormity and depth of the Bible. It's okay if we read just a verse or two today.

But more important than reading His words, we must choose to receive them. And even more important, we must live them. Because the more we apply God's teaching to our lives, the more it becomes part of us.

More important than reading His words, we must choose to receive them.

God's Word to me. God's Word in me. God's Word working through me. God's Word lived out by me. Let this be the rhythm of truth in my life.

Dear Lord, help me see You today in even the smallest ways. I admit sometimes I get really overwhelmed by the enormity and depth of the Bible, but I know You will give me eyes to see, ears to hear, and a heart to receive what I need for today. Give me the wisdom I need for what's on my plate today. In Jesus' name, amen.

16

When Things Get Worse Just Before They Get Better

"Everyone who hears these words of mine and puts them into practice is like a wise man who built his house on the rock."

Matthew 7:24

Over the last couple of years, I've watched my nearly thirty-year-old home undergo several renovation projects. Renovations are not for the faint of heart. The projects cause mess, the results are sometimes slow to take shape, and the process can feel never ending.

And with each floor that's torn up, wall that's removed, and plan that's put in motion—I'm paying attention. As I've seen portions of our home demolished beyond recognition and put back together again—I'm learning that home renovations are so very similar to heart renovations.

I've jotted down some important lessons I've collected from my renovation projects, and I want to pass them along from my journal to yours.

1. You have to tear some things down before you can build back up in new and beautiful ways.

It's impossible to see true transformation unless you remove the damaged and unhealthy portions first. Houses and people are alike in this way. Sometimes we have to work through what was so we can move on to what can be. This doesn't always mean that we have to remove people who don't want to cooperate with healthier patterns for our relationship. But it may mean that we create boundaries that clearly establish what behaviors are acceptable and what are not. Boundaries are not established to shove people away but rather so we hold ourselves together.

Sometimes we have to work through what was so we can move on to what can be.

2. Working on the foundation isn't the most appealing or attractive work, but it is some of the most important.

Jesus spoke of this truth in Matthew 7:24–27:

> *"Everyone who hears these words of mine and puts them into practice is like a wise man who built his house on the*

rock. The rain came down, the streams rose, and the winds blew and beat against that house; yet it did not fall, because it had its foundation on the rock. But everyone who hears these words of mine and does not put them into practice is like a foolish man who built his house on sand. The rain came down, the streams rose, and the winds blew and beat against that house, and it fell with a great crash."

Even though working on the foundation isn't the most glamorous part of construction, it is a crucial step we can't skip.

I love how Eugene Peterson paraphrased Matthew 7:24–25:

"These words I speak to you are not incidental additions to your life, homeowner improvements to your standard of living. They are foundational words, words to build a life on. If you work these words into your life, you are like a smart carpenter who built his house on solid rock. Rain poured down, the river flooded, a tornado hit—but nothing moved that house. It was fixed to the rock." (The Message)

Building our lives on anything but God's truth will result in a shaky foundation—a detriment to any building project before it even begins. We must put in the necessary, hard work of building our lives and our faith on the solid grounds of Scripture through the consistency of daily seeking God.

3. Not everyone is going to like what you're doing.

People criticize what they don't understand.

Change invites both compliments and criticism. Sometimes people criticize what they don't understand. My counselor, Jim, often tells me, "People are down on what they aren't up on." While change is good, people who don't like change will be the last to call it good. Just remember what comes out of someone else's mouth is a reflection of their heart, not yours.

4. It's good to stay humble enough to realize sometimes you need to get the professionals involved.

Some things you can do on your own, and some things you can't. Many small repairs can be handled without the help of a professional, but most large renovations that require more major work must be handled with care by those who are skilled and experienced. The same is true with the deeper emotional work in our lives. There are doctors, Christian counselors, and therapists trained to bring renewed health and restoration to both body and soul. My family and I have benefited greatly by bringing in the professionals in seasons when it was necessary, and we're so grateful we did.

5. Those who don't lose sight of the progress being made will find joy in the process.

And it's always a process. Renovations often make things worse during the tear-out and early construction phases before things start to get better and more beautiful. The same is true with healing the human heart.

Heart renovations, like home renovations, take diligence, patience, and a whole lot of prayer. But with God as our Master Carpenter, we can live assured in the process—we are a beautiful work in progress.

Track the progress you do see. Be patient with the setbacks. Celebrate the wins, even the small ones. Stacks of small wins turn into big wins. And eventually you'll be so glad you pressed through the renovation when you see the beauty that comes from all the hard work.

Renovations often make things worse before they get more beautiful. The same is true with the healing human heart.

God, help me have patience for the renovations You are doing in my heart. In the messy middle of the process, help me see the beauty that is taking shape and the joy that can be found even here in this season. In Jesus' name, amen.

17

The Blessings of Boundaries

The one who has knowledge uses words with restraint,
and whoever has understanding is even-tempered.

Proverbs 17:27

Have you ever found yourself having an out-of-control reaction in response to someone else's out-of-control actions?

I understand. It's all so very hard.

When I share biblical discernment with someone I love, but then they go away and do the opposite, it's maddening. My resulting reaction is not me being dramatic or overly emotional . . . I'm simply trying to save us both from the impending train wreck I can so obviously see headed our way!

A perfect example would be the two gallon-sized baggies stuffed full of ripped-up papers currently sitting on my dresser. Why do I have baggies of ripped papers? So glad you asked.

Some important documents came in the mail one day. In my defense, my name was included on the envelope. But the minute I opened the envelope and started reading through the contents, my blood pressure skyrocketed. One of my people was moving forward with something I deeply disagreed with. I had absolutely vocalized my many reasons to shut down this idea. I couldn't believe they weren't listening to me.

In hindsight, I should have simply reminded my family member of my boundary to not bail them out financially if this decision they were making was as detrimental as I thought it would be.

Instead, I just stood there in my kitchen and slowly tore the papers into as many tiny pieces as I could. I also tore the folders they were in and the mailing envelopes as well. I quietly stuffed all the mess into the baggies and sat them on the counter with a note that read, "This is all I have to say about this situation."

It felt so good in that moment. But the next morning I woke up and was like, *Really, Lysa?! Really?!* All my family member said back to me was, "Wow, you've made quite a statement." Now I was the one who needed to apologize and figure out a way to tell the company needing to now resend the papers that I had accidentally, on purpose, in a crazed moment, shredded. And when I did, the lady who worked at that company told me she'd recently read one of my books. Perfect. Wonderful. Ugh.

Controlling ourselves cannot be dependent on our efforts to control others.

I know I have hyperextended my capacity when I shift from calm words to angry tirades. I shift from blessing to cursing. I shift from peace to chaos. I shift from discussing the papers to ripping them to shreds and putting them in baggies.

What do I need to do in response to situations that feel so out of control that they make me lose my self-control?

Controlling ourselves cannot be dependent on our efforts to control others.

Establish boundaries. I mentioned this next sentence in the previous devotion, but it's worth repeating: Boundaries aren't to push others away. Boundaries are to help hold me together.

The truth is, without good boundaries, other people's poor choices will bankrupt your spiritual capacity for compassion. Not to mention the fact that at some point you will get so exhausted and worn down, you will lose your self-control because they are so out of control. You'll sacrifice your peace on the altar of their chaos. Soon you will get swept into a desperate urgency to get them to stop! Right! Now! And we all know acts of desperation hold hands with degradation. I'm preaching to myself because I've got the tendency to downgrade who I really am in moments of utter frustration and exhaustion when I don't keep appropriate boundaries.

It all makes me think of today's key verse: *"The one who has knowledge uses words with restraint, and whoever has understanding is even-tempered"* (Proverbs 17:27).

When we understand that only God can bring about true change in another person's heart and life, it frees us from all of our panic-induced attempts to control them. We can love them. Pray for them. Try to share godly wisdom with them. But we don't have to downgrade our gentleness to hastily spoken words of anger and resentment. We don't have to downgrade our attitude for reconciliation to acts of retaliation. We can use our words with restraint and stay even-tempered because we're ultimately entrusting them to the Lord.

I know this isn't easy, sweet friend. But it is wisdom.

It's for the sake of our sanity that we draw necessary boundaries. It's for the sake of stability that we stay consistent with those boundaries. And it's with a heart of humility that maintaining those boundaries becomes a possibility.

Lord, please forgive me for all of the times I've tried to step into Your place in the lives of the people I love. Today I'm releasing them into Your hands. You are their Savior, not me. Show me anywhere I need to draw healthy boundary lines, and help me maintain them with humility and love. In Jesus' Name, Amen.

18

Where Is My Happily Ever After?

"Seek first his kingdom and his righteousness, and all these things will be given to you as well. Therefore do not worry about tomorrow, for tomorrow will worry about itself. Each day has enough trouble of its own."

Matthew 6:33–34

I feel the most unsettled when I'm uncertain about the future. I suspect many of you are also facing circumstances that have left you feeling caught off guard and unsure about what tomorrow holds. So many times I find myself bracing for impact when I check my daily news feed. If there's one word that seems most certain to describe the times we are living in, it's *uncertain*.

Maybe you're in a job where you feel unsettled, and you think that God is leading you somewhere else, but He hasn't yet revealed what's next. So, for now, you walk into an office every day giving it your all, but your heart feels disconnected and your real calling unfulfilled.

Or maybe you've been watching everyone else in your life find love, walk down the aisle, and start the life you've dreamed of. Then a few months ago you met someone who was everything you've been hoping for. You told your friends this might be the one. And then this week you felt that person pulling back. It's hard to understand. You feel panicked. But the more you press in, the more distance you feel between the two of you.

There are thousands of scenarios that evoke these feelings of uncertainty, fear, and exhaustion from life not being like you thought it would be.

Sometimes you just have to walk in your "I don't know."

Whatever your situation is, you probably feel like you can't change it, but you still have to live through the realities of what's happening right now. Sometimes you just have to walk in your "I don't know."

The Lord makes it clear in His Word that things will not always go as we wish they would in this life. Here are the quotes we so often hear:

"In this world you will have trouble." (John 16:33)

"Each day has enough trouble of its own." (Matthew 6:34)

All this trouble is exhausting. Walking in the "I don't know" is scary. And sometimes we can be desperate to make things easier than they really are.

We keep thinking if we can just get through this circumstance, life will settle down and finally the words *happily ever after* will scroll across the glorious scene of us skipping happily into the sunset.

But what if life settling down and all your disappointments going away would be the worst thing that could happen to you?

What if your "I don't know" is helping you, not hurting you?

Remember those verses we just read about troubles? Here they are again in the context of the full passages:

> *"I have told you these things, so that in me you may have peace. In this world you will have trouble. But take heart! I have overcome the world."* (John 16:33)

> *"Seek first his kingdom and his righteousness, and all these things will be given to you as well. Therefore do not worry about tomorrow, for tomorrow will worry about itself. Each day has enough trouble of its own."* (Matthew 6:33–34)

The crucial detail for us to have peace in the middle of everything we face is to stay close to the Lord.

We think we want comfort in the I-don't-know times of life. But comfort isn't a solution to seek; rather, it's a byproduct we'll reap when we stay close to the Lord.

I wish I could promise you that everything's going to turn out like you're hoping it will. I can't, of course. But what I can

Comfort isn't a solution to seek; rather, it's a byproduct we'll reap when we stay close to the Lord.

promise you is this: God is close to us even in our "I don't knows." God has lessons for us that are crucially important for our future, and we're learning them in the middle of our "I don't knows." God has a strength He must prepare us with, and the training ground is here in the "I don't know."

This time isn't a waste, and it's definitely not pointless when we are walking with God.

Let's cry out to God, declaring that this hard time will be a holy time, a close-to-God time. And let's choose to believe that there is good happening, even in these places. Because wherever God is, good is being worked.

Father God, more than I need You to fix anything in my life, I just need You. I am declaring this hard time as a holy time. Help me live in such a way that marks this season by closeness with You. In Jesus' name, amen.

A Letter from Lysa

If ever there is a day you hang your head because of something not nice or not true someone said about you, remember this: prove them wrong.

You are kind.

You are fun.

You are loved.

You are thoughtful.

You are prayerful.

Don't fall into the trap of saying ugly things back. Don't retaliate. Take the higher ground—and because you don't have to live with reaction regret, celebrate.

Now you go live in such a way that illuminates the beautiful reality of who you are and who Jesus is in you. People will eventually see the truth.

Lysa

19

When Giving Grace Feels Hard

Let your speech always be gracious, seasoned with salt, so that you may know how you ought to answer each person.

Colossians 4:6 ESV

Sometimes God's Word can feel like an impossible order, don't you think? Take today's passage for example: Paul told us we are to let our words be gracious. The NIV actually reads "full of grace." Full of it. As in, the bulk of our words should be made up of grace toward the person with whom we are conversing.

Not partial grace. Not halfway grace. All-the-way grace.

I don't know if you've ever tried this, but it's hard.

It's hard when one of the precious people living in your house does something irresponsible for the tenth time! It's hard when a trusted friend deeply wounds you. And it's incredibly hard when people share their thoughts and opinions so freely and carelessly on social media, leaving you feeling frustrated, angry, or even personally attacked.

I don't know about you, but words laced with grace aren't typically the first ones that come to mind when someone's hurtful words have landed like daggers in my heart. I want to defend myself. And point out how they're misunderstanding my intentions.

But just because speaking with grace is hard doesn't mean it's impossible. And Paul's words to the Colossians remind us that our words matter.

Paul specifically wanted us to consider our words in light of unbelievers, telling us in Colossians 4:5–6 (ESV), *"Walk in wisdom toward outsiders, making the best use of the time. Let your speech always be gracious, seasoned with salt, so that you may know how you ought to answer each person."*

Our words matter.

And look at how Jesus modeled grace and truth in John 1:14, which says, *"The Word became flesh and made his dwelling among us. We have seen his glory, the glory of the one and only Son, who came from the Father, full of grace and truth."* Every instance in the New Testament where we see grace and truth together is always connected to Jesus.

We are to be people of truth with grace-filled words. People who choose healing and helpful words. Because whether we realize it or not, believers and unbelievers alike are listening intently to the words we speak. They're reading the words we type. And our words testify to the kind of relationship we have with Jesus and the kind of effect He has on our hearts.

So where is the hope in the midst of words that make our

pulses race and our faces flush? How do we keep our words full of grace?

We remember that Jesus doesn't offer us partial grace. He doesn't offer us halfway grace. Jesus gave, and continues to give, all-the-way grace. Grace that took Him all the way to the cross.

Oh, how we need to let this truth interrupt us and redirect us. The divine grace we receive from Christ should fuel our gracious natures and fill our conversations. Because we are people who desperately need grace, we should be people who lavishly give grace.

Jesus doesn't offer us partial grace . . . He gave grace that took Him all the way to the cross.

And not only are we to be gracious in our speech, Paul also told us our words should be "seasoned with salt." In rabbinic tradition, this phrase would have been associated with wisdom. In Greco-Roman literature, it meant to be "winsome or witty" in speech. Paul was reminding the Colossians they were called to be people filled with godly wisdom. To be able to respond to objections to the gospel in a manner that was winsome. He wanted their words, and ours, to attract people to Christ, not repel them.

I don't know who puts grace to the test in your life. But I do know the Holy Spirit is willing to help us choose grace-filled words, if only we will pause long enough for Him to replace the first ones that may pop into our brains.

But even before that, we can also pre-decide that today, because of the lavish grace of Jesus, we will choose the way of grace. With His help, we can speak with honor in the midst of being dishonored. We can speak with peace in the midst of being threatened. We can speak of good things in the midst of bad situations.

Oh Lord, may this be true of us. May our words reflect that we know Jesus, love Jesus, and spend time with Jesus.

Father God, I want to pause for a moment and thank You for Your Son, Jesus. He could have held back His grace. But instead, He chose to pour out every single drop for me on the cross. So remind me that I give grace because I so desperately need it, even when it feels super hard and honestly sometimes undeserved with people I'm in relationships with. In Jesus' name, amen.

20

Forgiveness: The Double-Edged Word

Be kind to one another, tenderhearted, forgiving one another, as God in Christ forgave you.

Ephesians 4:32 ESV

Do you ever find yourself defining life by before and after the deep hurt?

The horrific season. The conversation that stunned you. The shocking day of discovery. The divorce. The wrongful death so unfathomable you still can't believe they are gone. The breakup. The day your friend walked away. The hateful conversation. The remark that seems to now be branded on your soul. The day everything changed.

That marked moment in time. Life before. Life now. Is it even possible to move on from something like this? Is it even possible to create a life that's beautiful again?

I deeply understand this kind of defining devastation in such a personal way. Like you, I wish I didn't have such an intimate understanding of those feelings. But I do.

If you've read my book *It's Not Supposed to Be This Way*, you know of the shattering discovery of my husband Art's affair and the long road of uncertainty I was still walking at the end of that book. The years of hellish heartbreak that followed the discovery did eventually take an unexpected turn toward reconciliation. I'm grateful, but as I've shared with you already in these pages, I have not been spared the slow and grueling work of finding your way again after experiencing something that forever marks your life.

When your heart has been shattered and reshaped into something that doesn't quite feel normal inside your own chest yet, the word *forgiveness* feels a bit unrealistic to bring into the conversation.

But, friend, can I whisper to you something I'm learning? Without requiring anything from you, but rather offering you an invitation into the process with me today?

Forgiveness is possible, but it won't always feel possible.

It's a double-edged word, isn't it?

It's hard to give. It's amazing to get. But when we receive forgiveness so freely from the Lord and refuse to give it, something heavy starts to form in our souls.

It's the weight of forgiveness that wasn't allowed to pass through me. That's mainly because I've misunderstood something so incredibly profound about forgiveness.

Unforgiveness is that heavy feeling in my soul because I didn't let the forgiveness that flowed to me, flow through me.

Unforgiveness is that heavy feeling in my soul because I didn't let the forgiveness that flowed to me, flow through me.

Forgiveness isn't something hard we have the option to do or not do. Forgiveness is something hard-won that we have the opportunity to participate in.

Our part in forgiveness isn't one of desperation where we have to muscle through with gritted teeth and clenched fists. It isn't sobbing through the resistance of all our justifications to stay angry and hurt and horrified by all they did. This is what I once thought forgiveness was, and after already being the one who was hurt, I couldn't imagine having yet another process to work through.

But when I wrongly think forgiveness rises and falls on all my efforts, conjured maturity, bossed-around resistance, and gentle feelings that feel real one moment and fake the next, I'll never be able to authentically give the kind of forgiveness Jesus has given me.

My ability to forgive others rises and falls by leaning into what Jesus has already done, which allows His grace for me to flow freely through me (Ephesians 4:7).

Forgiveness isn't an act of my determination.

Forgiveness is only made possible by my cooperation.

Cooperation is what I've been missing. Cooperation with what Jesus has already done makes verses like Ephesians 4:32 possible. *"Be kind to one another, tenderhearted, forgiving one another, as God in Christ forgave you"* (ESV).

Forgiving one another just as Christ forgave you. God knew we couldn't do it on our own. So He made a way not dependent on our strength. A forgiving way. A way to grab on to Jesus' outstretched arms, bloody from crucifixion and dripping with redemption. He forgives what we could never be good enough to make right. And makes a way for us to simply cooperate with His work of forgiveness . . . for us to receive and for us to give.

That person or people—they've caused enough pain for you, for me, and for those around us. There's been enough damage done. And you don't have to be held hostage by the pain. You get to decide how you'll move forward. If you're knee-deep in pain and resonate with the feelings of resistance I have felt too, let me assure you: Forgiveness is possible. And it is good.

So I want you to just sit here for a moment and consider the possibility around this double-edged word, *forgiveness.* Not because your pain doesn't matter. Not because what they did was right. Not because it fixes everything. But because your heart is much too beautiful a place

Your heart is much too beautiful a place for unhealed pain.

for unhealed pain. Your soul is much too deserving of freedom to stay stuck here.

God, thank You for caring about my pain and not leaving me alone in hard situations I face. Show me how I can cooperate with forgiveness today. Help me continue to take steps in this healing journey. In Jesus' name, amen.

21

Please Don't Give Me a Christian Answer

Jesus wept.

John 11:35

I love Jesus. I love God. I love His truth. I love people.

But I don't love packaged Christian answers. Those that tie everything up in a nice, neat bow and make life a little too tidy. Because there just isn't anything tidy about some awful and sad and so incredibly evil things that happen in our broken world.

And God help me if I think I'm going to make things better by thinking up a clever Christian saying to add to all the dialogue. God certainly doesn't need people like me—with limited perspectives, limited understanding, and limited depth—trying to make sense of things that just don't make sense.

Is there a place for God's truth in all this? Absolutely. But we must, must, must let God direct us. In His time. In His way. In His love.

And when things are awful, perhaps we should just say,

"This is awful." When things don't make sense, we can't shy away from simply saying, "This doesn't make sense." Because there is a difference between a wrong word at the wrong time and a right word at the right time.

When things are awful, perhaps we should just say, "This is awful."

When my sister died a horribly tragic death, it was because a doctor prescribed some medication no child should ever be given. And it set off a chain of events that eventually found my family standing over a pink, rose-draped casket.

Weeping.

Hurting.

Needing time to wrestle with grief and anger and loss.

And it infuriated my raw soul when people tried to sweep up the shattered pieces of our life by saying things like, "Well, God just needed another angel in heaven." Besides being off theologically, statements like that took the shards of my grief and twisted them even more deeply into my already broken heart.

I understand why they said things like this. They wanted to say something—anything—to make it better. Their compassion compelled them to come close.

And I wanted them there. And then I didn't.

Everything was a contradiction. I could be crying hysterically one minute and laughing the next. And then I'd feel so awful for daring to laugh that I wanted to cuss. And then sing a praise song. I wanted to shake my fist at God and then read His Scriptures for hours.

There's just nothing tidy about all that.

But the thing I know now that I wish I knew then is that Jesus understands what it is like to deeply feel human emotions like grief and heartache. We see this in John 11:32–35 when Jesus received the news His dear friend Lazarus had died:

> *When Mary reached the place where Jesus was and saw him, she fell at his feet and said, "Lord, if you had been here, my brother [Lazarus] would not have died." When Jesus saw her weeping, and the Jews who had come along with her also weeping, he was deeply moved in spirit and troubled.*
>
> *"Where have you laid him?" he asked.*
>
> *"Come and see, Lord," they replied.*
>
> *Jesus wept.*

Yes, Jesus wept and mourned with His loved ones in that devastatingly heartbreaking moment. And the fact that He can identify with my pain is so comforting to me. He meets us in our grief. And we can bring the hope He promises and the

Jesus understands what it is like to deeply feel human emotions like grief and heartbreak.

comfort He supplies when others are grieving too.

You want to know the best thing someone said to me in the middle of my grief?

I was standing in the midst of all the tears falling down on black dresses and black suits on that gray funeral day. My heels were sinking into the grass. I was staring down at an ant pile. The ants were running like mad around a footprint that had squashed their home.

I was wondering if I stood in that pile and let them sting me a million times if maybe that pain would distract me from my soul pain. At least I knew how to soothe physical pain.

Suddenly this little pigtailed girl skipped by me and exclaimed, "I hate ants."

And that was hands-down the best thing anyone said that day. Because she just entered in right where I was. Noticed where I was focused in that moment and just said something basic. Normal. Obvious.

Yes, there is a place for a solid Christian answer from well-intentioned friends. Absolutely. But then there's also a place to weep with a hurting friend from the depths of your soul. A time when there really aren't any words that can help the pain.

God, help us to know the difference.

Dear Lord, I know You are the only One who can bring comfort to seemingly impossible situations. Thank You for comforting me in my pain so that I can comfort others in their pain. In Jesus' name, amen.

22

When God Gives You More Than You Can Handle

Indeed, we felt we had received the sentence of death. But this happened that we might not rely on ourselves but on God, who raises the dead.

2 Corinthians 1:9

Have you ever heard the statement, "God won't give you more than you can handle"?

As I type these words, I know I'm not the only one who feels they've been given more than they can bear at times.

I felt this deeply when I was diagnosed with cancer, and like I told you about in an earlier devotion, I was already in an incredibly hard season. It felt like some sort of awful mistake. I had no family history of breast cancer. I was young(ish) and healthy.

And yet there I was thinking, *God . . . this definitely feels like more than I can handle.*

God does say He won't allow us to be tempted beyond what we can bear and that He always provides a way out (1 Corinthians

10:13). But that's not the same as God not giving us more than we can handle.

God didn't cause my cancer. But He did allow it. And He sometimes will allow more and more. The world is filled with people who are dealt more than they can handle. And, surprisingly, the Bible is filled with them too.

God didn't cause my cancer. But He did allow it.

The apostle Paul wrote:

> *We do not want you to be uninformed, brothers and sisters, about the troubles we experienced in the province of Asia. We were under great pressure, far beyond our ability to endure, so that we despaired of life itself. Indeed, we felt we had received the sentence of death. But this happened that we might not rely on ourselves but on God, who raises the dead.* (2 Corinthians 1:8–9)

No, God doesn't expect us to handle this. He wants us to hand this over to Him.

He doesn't want us to rally more of our own strength. He wants us to rely solely on His strength.

If we keep walking around, thinking God won't give us more than we can handle, we set ourselves up to be suspicious of God. We know we're facing things that are too much for us.

After my diagnosis, I had some really difficult days. I needed

God doesn't expect us to handle this. He wants us to hand this over to Him.

God to show me His perspective so I could set my perspective. But it didn't come right away. And that frustrated me. I was filled with fear and questions like, *Why this? Why now? Why me?*

The story I started telling myself was that life would never get any better.

But thinking about everything I didn't know wasn't getting me anywhere. So I started listing things I did know. And the main thing I know? I know God is good. I didn't know the details of God's good plan, but I could make His goodness the starting place to renew my perspective.

So now let me tell the story of the recent events in my life using God's goodness as the central theme. Had things not blown up in my marriage a few months beforehand, I never would have hit the pause button on life to go get a mammogram. But because I had a mammogram at that exact time, the doctors caught a cancer that needed to be caught. And because they caught a cancer that needed to be caught, I had every fighting chance to beat this cancer.

By God's grace, I am living today cancer-free. I am so thankful and relieved and deeply moved by all the prayers that carried me through that season.

So today if you find yourself with something in front of you that feels like more than you can handle, please know I am praying for you. I am praying for you as you battle through tough stuff. Whether your situation is cancer or not, we all have circumstances that feel impossibly hard.

You see, we're all living out a story, but then there's the story we tell ourselves. We just need to make sure we're telling ourselves the right story. Yes, God will give us more than we can handle. But He always has eventual good in mind.

We don't have to like it, but maybe knowing this can help us live through it.

Dear Lord, I'm choosing to hand over to You today all the things I don't understand. It feels overwhelming, but I am declaring Your goodness over each of those situations today. Intercept the stories I'm telling myself that don't line up with this truth. In Jesus' name, amen.

23

An Unexpected Thread of Hope

Purge me with hyssop, and I shall be clean;
wash me, and I shall be whiter than snow.

Psalm 51:7 ESV

The consequences of sin can be devastating. King David knew this truth firsthand.

Psalm 51 was written by David after he was confronted about an adulterous affair he had with a woman named Bathsheba. David was horrified by just how far from God his sin had taken him. There were consequences that could never be undone. Bathsheba's husband, Uriah, was killed. And the baby Bathsheba had conceived with David (during the affair) died.

This man after God's own heart (1 Samuel 13:14) was utterly disappointed in himself, but he did exactly what we all need to do. He brought his sin and his pain to God. He invited hope into a situation he could have easily labeled hopeless. I believe God wants us to know today we still have hope in the midst of our problems too.

Psalm 51 is such a beautiful example of a broken man in

need of hope turning to God with confession, repentance, and in humility, asking for help. In Psalm 51:7, our key verse for today, David mentioned a very specific plant when he prayed, *"Purge me with hyssop, and I shall be clean; wash me, and I shall be whiter than snow"* (ESV). The first time I read this I remember thinking, whenever the Bible mentions something specifically by name, like the hyssop here, it's interesting to see why God so intentionally allowed that detail to be revealed. I wondered, *Where else is hyssop specifically mentioned in Scripture?* The answer was fascinating. Hyssop is a plant covered with beautiful purple flowers. And it shows up at some of the most profound moments throughout Bible history. It's like a purple thread of hope woven throughout Scripture:

What might happen today if we invite God's hope into a situation we've already labeled hopeless?

1. Hyssop was the paintbrush at Passover in Exodus 12:22.

In Exodus, we read about the problems placed on the children of Israel. Due to a chain of events set off by the jealousy of a few brothers (Genesis 27), the Israelites eventually ended up being held captive in Egypt. God sent Moses to ask Pharaoh to set His people free, but Pharaoh's heart was hardened. Many plagues were then sent, but it wasn't until God sent the plague of striking down the firstborn of both human and animal families that Pharaoh changed his mind.

But in order for God to pass over the firstborn of the children of Israel, He told them they must paint the doorframes of their homes with the blood of a lamb. And the tool He asked them to use was very specific—a bunch of hyssop.

2. Hyssop was the purification tool in Psalm 51:7.

David cried out to God and asked Him to use hyssop to deal with the problems within him.

Why hyssop?

A quick look at Leviticus 14 reveals hyssop was used for people with leprosy—those affected with a skin condition that caused them to be ostracized and placed outside of the city.

David was essentially someone needing to be cleansed. Remember, sin separates us from God. Just like people with infectious skin conditions were separated, so are we when we sin. We are outside of the will of God when we live with an unrepentant heart.

David needed God to cleanse him from his sin within, and

so do we. Which ties in with the last encounter with hyssop we're going to talk about.

3. Hyssop was present when Jesus became the promise fulfilled in John 19:29.

If we turn over to John 19, we will see hyssop is one of the last things Jesus interacted with on this earth.

As Jesus hung on the cross, He said He was thirsty. Then, in John 19:29, we're told, *"A jar full of sour wine stood there, so they put a sponge full of the sour wine on a hyssop branch and held it to his mouth"* (ESV). Then He declared, *"It is finished,"* and breathed His last breath (v. 30).

I love how hyssop weaves all of these moments together and points us straight to the hope we have in Jesus. Hyssop was there as the paintbrush at Passover. Hyssop was there as the purification tool of David. And it was there when Jesus became the ultimate Passover Lamb, providing the way for us to be cleansed and purified from all sin.

Oh, how I pray we will let this purple thread weave hope into our stories today. Jesus is the answer to the problems placed on us and the problems found within us. And when we know we are never a people without hope, we can always see beautiful ahead of us.

Lord Jesus, we bring our every problem and need to You today, knowing You are the answer. Thank You for the hope we have in You because of the victory you won at the cross. In Jesus' name, amen.

24

A Script to Preach to Myself

They triumphed over him by the blood of the Lamb and by the word of their testimony.

Revelation 12:11

I'll never forget the first time a girl in elementary school told me I was ugly.

I remember it felt like the world stopped spinning and suddenly everyone was looking in my direction nodding in agreement. Red-hot shame filled my cheeks. I ran to the bathroom. I stared at my face in the mirror. I didn't bother to wipe away the tears and snot. I just stood there wishing I could cover up whatever it was that made that girl determine I wasn't acceptable.

But I realized, it wasn't just a part of me that she thought was ugly. It was the sum total of me. In her estimation, I was ugly. Not just my hair or my nose or my body . . . it was all of me. And the saddest part of all . . . I agreed with her.

It's been decades since that unfortunate incident that said way more about that other little girl's issues than mine. But I can still find myself staring into the mirror agreeing with statements that are so opposite of God's truth. We know the enemy is the father of lies (John 8:44). But where I get tripped up is when my insecurities make his lies feel like the loudest truth in my head.

That's why we have to set our minds and our hearts on the absolute truth of God's Word. When our insecurities beg us to believe "we aren't beautifully and wonderfully made," we must look to the hope-filled pages of Scripture to remind us of the difference between lies and truth.

The enemy wants you to stare and compare in all the ways you already feel inadequate. He wants you to doubt God's goodness in how He made you. So, if you start hearing the enemy's script, recognize it for what it is: false accusations.

Here's a cheat sheet to remind you how he whispers in your ear:

"If only you were . . ."
"You aren't enough . . ."
"You are too much . . ."
"If God really loved you . . ."
"People think you're so . . ."
"Why can't you just . . ."
"Why does she always get . . ."
"Why can't you ever . . ."

Sweet friend, don't help the enemy get you into a state of defeat by believing and repeating his scripts. God will lead you with love and conviction but never accusation or condemnation. He isn't measuring you by what you are or aren't accomplishing or what size your jeans are or how your kids are behaving today or how much money you have in your bank account. He loves your heart. He wants your heart. Reject the lies and start listening to the One who knows you completely and loves you fully.

Let's start preaching God's truth to our hearts in the midst of whatever insecurities are taunting us today. It is the most powerful way to help us fight the lies and accusations of the enemy. We will defeat him by the blood of the Lamb and by the word of our testimony (Revelation 12:11, paraphrase).

God will lead you with love and conviction but never accusation or condemnation.

Oh, how I love that last verse.

God's message of hell-defeating hope is often most powerfully preached from the lips of those whose pain has been turned into the purpose of telling people about what God has done in their lives.

Jesus has brought the blood. We can bring the words of our testimony.

Also, never forget who is the "*accuser of our brothers and*

Jesus has brought the blood. We can bring the words of our testimony.

sisters" (Revelation 12:10) and that his vicious lies will always go after your most vulnerable insecurities and doubts.

We must let God's words become *the* words we live by. Let's change the scripts begging us to believe anything opposite of God's truth.

He is with you, He will not leave you, and He absolutely will see you all the way through this.

God, help me seek You alone to tell me who I am when I am tempted to believe lies about myself. Today I am choosing to flip the script and preach truth to myself. I know You love me, You won't leave me, and You will absolutely see me through whatever I am facing right now. In Jesus' name, amen.

A Letter from Lysa

Dear friend,

We have today. Even with all the ups and downs and unexpected situations, it's a gift. Such a precious gift.

Loss teaches us that. And gives us a new way to see—a new way to be.

Wrap your arms around someone you love and savor the privilege of saying, "I'm so grateful you're here right now. I love you to the moon and a million times more." And then do it again.

Let things get a little messy and see it as rich evidence of life.

Let things get a little loud and listen as if it's the most beautiful melody.

Let things be a little silly sometimes and dare to giggle and play along.

And throw confetti just to celebrate an ordinary day. After all, each day is truly extraordinary in its own little way.

Lysa

25

Higher Perspective in Present Realities

"For I know the plans I have for you, declares the Lord, plans for welfare and not for evil, to give you a future and a hope."

Jeremiah 29:11 ESV

Longsuffering isn't a word I want to be part of my story. It means having or showing patience despite troubles. And I don't particularly want troubles to begin with, let alone for any extended period of time.

Thankfully, today's passage of Scripture offers us encouragement for when we're not sure we can endure our season of suffering for one more second.

In Jeremiah 29, the children of Israel got news from the prophet Jeremiah that they were going to be held in captivity by Babylon for seventy years. Think about how long seventy years is. If we had to go to prison today for seventy years, for most of us that would mean we'd probably die in captivity. Seventy years feels impossibly long, incredibly unfair, and horribly hard. It would seem like a lifetime of hardship without a lifeline of hope.

But here's what God told the people of Israel: *"When seventy years are completed for Babylon, I will visit you, and I will fulfill to you my promise and bring you back to this place"* (v. 10 ESV).

This is the scene and the setting where we then get these familiar and glorious promises I love to cling to:

> *"For I know the plans I have for you, declares the Lord, plans for welfare and not for evil, to give you a future and a hope. Then you will call upon me and come and pray to me, and I will hear you. You will seek me and find me, when you seek me with all your heart. I will be found by you."* (vv. 11–14 ESV)

God is assuring His people that His thoughts and intentions toward them are fixed and established. His plans are for their "welfare" not for hurt. His sure and steady promise is one of restoration.

But He also reminds them of what they must do as they await the fulfillment of His promise. They need to call on Him. They need to intentionally and wholeheartedly seek Him.

When we seek God, we see God. We don't see His physical form, but we see

His sure and steady promise is one of restoration.

Him at work and can start to see more of what He sees. Trust grows. If our hearts are willing to trust Him, He will entrust to us more of His perspective.

If we want to see Him in our circumstances and see His perspective, we must seek Him, His ways, and His Word. That's where we find His good plans and promises for hope and a future.

If we find ourselves in an incredibly disappointing place—a place we don't want to be—it's easy to start feeling that some of God's good plans don't apply to us. We can even lapse into the mentality that we somehow slipped through the cracks of God's good plans.

But the truth is, God is closer than we often realize. Like I've stated before, He sees things we don't see, and He knows things we don't know. He has a perspective from where He is that allows Him to see all things—the past, the present, and the future—from the day we were conceived to the day we breathe our last breath, and even beyond that into eternity. He declares He is our rescuer. He is the One who will sustain us. And He is more than able to bring His plans to pass (Isaiah 46:3–11).

Just remember, not yet doesn't mean not ever.

All these things were true for the Israelites. And they're true for us.

For the Israelites, the news that they

would be in captivity for seventy years was absolute reality. But the truth that God had a good plan and a purpose not to harm them but to give them a future and a hope—that promise was very much in process all the while they were in captivity.

Don't rush past that last sentence too quickly. God's promises for you are in process as well. Right now. Even in circumstances you can't see any evidence of good yet. Just remember "not yet" doesn't mean "not ever."

Let's cry out to Him in the midst of our suffering. Let's earnestly seek Him and ask Him to help us look at our circumstances through the lens of certainty in who He is even when we are uncertain about how things will work out. We are not forgotten. And our longsuffering won't seem nearly as long or nearly as painful when we know God's perspective is to use every single second of our suffering for good.

Father God, thank You for reminding me I can trust You in the waiting. Thank You for being present even in these moments. I know You will carry me through, and I trust You in the process. In Jesus' name, amen.

26

A New Way to Walk and a New Way to See

When Jesus saw him lying there and learned that he had been in this condition for a long time, he asked him, "Do you want to get well?"

John 5:6

I walked into my appointment with my counselor, Jim, wishing I'd canceled.

So much felt unsettled in my life. At this point in our journey, not only were Art and I separated, but there were also layers of complicated realities that prevented us from being able to sit down and process the fallout after his affair.

As I sat in Jim's office, I felt utterly unmotivated to talk and overly motivated to cry.

"Lysa, do you have the desire to heal from this?"

I nodded my head yes. I did want to heal. From the marital devastation. From the shock of all the unpredictable ways people had reacted to what happened.

But how could I possibly start healing when there was no resolution or restitution or reconciliation with Art or others who had hurt me?

I thought those who did wrong things would realize they were wrong. And then surely they would say they were sorry and seek to make things right between us. Then I would consider forgiveness. And then I could possibly heal.

As Jim kept talking, I started to realize I might never feel like things were fair. Even if the people who hurt me suddenly became repentant and owned all they'd done, that wouldn't undo what had happened. That wouldn't instantly heal me or make any of this feel right.

Therefore, I had to separate my healing from their choices. My ability to heal cannot depend on anyone's choices but my own.

It reminded me of something I learned during a trip to the Holy Land when my guide taught about the only two healing miracles Jesus performed in Jerusalem.

My ability to heal cannot depend on anyone's choices but my own.

The first was a healing at the pools of Bethesda.

In John 5, we read about a lame man who thought he needed the cooperation of other people to help him get to the water when the angels stirred it, according to the superstition believed by many. So when Jesus came and asked him the question we find in our key verse—*"Do you want to be healed?"*—the man's response was surprising. He gave Jesus an excuse based on the fact that no one would help him into the water.

Isn't it amazing that the man was so focused on what others needed to do that he almost missed what Jesus could do?

Without one word about the other people, Jesus instructed him to get up, pick up his mat, and walk. The Bible then says, *"At once the man was cured"* (v. 9). The healing didn't involve anyone but the paralyzed man and Jesus.

The other healing miracle is found in John 9 with a blind man. In this story, we find the disciples wanting to know whose actions caused this man's blindness. Surely someone was at fault.

But Jesus blew that assumption apart. He didn't place blame or shame on anyone. He said this man's blindness *"happened so that the works of God might be displayed in him"* (v. 3). Jesus then spat onto the ground, mixed up some mud, rubbed it onto the blind man's eyes, then instructed him to go and wash in the pool of Siloam. Notice that Jesus didn't make healing contingent on other people doing or owning anything.

Jesus gave the instruction. The blind man obeyed. Jesus healed. The blind man moved forward.

My guide in Jerusalem that day said "one of these miracles

showed us a new way to walk and the other showed us a new way to see."

I couldn't grab my journal to record this revelation fast enough. I wrote, "For me to move forward, for me to see beyond this current darkness, is between me and the Lord. I don't need to wait on others to do anything. I must simply obey what God is asking of me right now. God has given me a new way to walk. And God has given me a new way to see. It's forgiveness. And it is beautiful."

Oh, friend, what if we stopped waiting for things to feel right and fair and placed our healing in the hands of Jesus instead?

Our ability to heal cannot depend on others wanting our forgiveness, but only on our willingness to give it.

Our ability to heal also cannot depend on them receiving adequate consequences for their disobedience, but only on our obedience to trust God's justice whether we ever see it or not.

My healing is my choice. And your healing? It's with the utmost compassion that I say your healing is your choice too.

I know how incredibly hard all of this is. But I'm finding what I learned both in Israel and in my counselor's office to be true.

We *can* heal. We *can* forgive. We *can* trust God. And none of those beautiful realities can be held hostage by another person.

My healing is my choice.

Lord, thank You for inviting me to see and walk in a new, healed way today. Forgiveness and healing may feel incredibly hard to choose sometimes, but I know that You give me the strength to walk through these processes. Thank You for making me more like You. In Jesus' name, amen.

27

When the Only Thing You Have Left to Give Is Time

Be gracious to me, O Lord, for I am languishing; heal me, O Lord, for my bones are troubled. My soul also is greatly troubled. But you, O Lord—how long?

Psalm 6:2–3 ESV

I love today's passage because it's a prayer first offered up by someone who knows the pain of *languishing*. That's not a word I use often, but it's actually the perfect word to describe what I felt during the years of great pain and uncertainty about my marriage.

Many people ask why I stayed and fought for my marriage. The answer to that is as complicated and intricate as trying to understand what makes the ocean pull back and stop at the shore.

As I've talked about before, there was a season when it wasn't reasonable or responsible to stay, so there were long stretches of separation in our journey. Just like when the ocean doesn't respect the boundary of the shoreline and hurricane conditions force evacuations.

But then the shoreline became safe again. And I had a choice.

To say I wrestled through fears of being hurt again is an understatement. There was also so much pain and damage done that it felt like trying again was harder than walking away. Our journey had lasted so long with so many dashed hopes along the way that I just didn't know if I had anything left to give.

So I gave the only thing I could—and that was time.

I made the decision to let some time pass and just observe how committed Art was to pursuing healing, whether or not I was open to him pursuing me. And I sought out wise advice from trusted friends who had been through life-altering heartbreaks and were now walking in healing. No matter what trauma or difficult issues you are facing, here are three pieces of wisdom those friends gave me that were truly helpful:

1. "Trust is built with time plus believable behavior."

My counselor taught me this, and it took the pressure off of me to feel like I had to figure everything out. I just had to pay attention to choices Art was making, what the Lord was saying to me in my daily time in His Word, and how my own healing was going. I was honest during this season about both my progress and my setbacks. My emotions got triggered, and I often wanted to talk about what I was experiencing. And honestly, the very best gauge I had was Art's reaction. If he was patient and understanding, it built my confidence that his heart was in a tender place.

2. "He will either be in recovery or relapse."

A wise friend of mine who knew how addictions can complicate healing situations shared this with me. It isn't as clear-cut in some situations, but for me, I could tell by his daily choices. The choices that someone makes often point to the habits they are establishing for their life moving forward. Healthy choices become habits that become healthy patterns that become a healthy life of recovery. My part in all of this is to always be honest about what I'm seeing . . . health or unhealth. Recovery or relapse. This isn't to put a label on someone, but rather to honestly gauge how to move forward.

3. "Lysa, what do you ultimately want?"

This simple question also proved incredibly helpful during this season. My answer was that I wanted to be able to enjoy simple moments again. And if that's what I wanted, I had to make choices that fed peace into my life rather than constantly jumping on the emotionally charged opportunities that are often presented in moments of relational crisis. I didn't do this perfectly, but I did do it intentionally. I intentionally chose not to take the bait Satan often offered me to say cutting remarks, pile on shame, or present myself as the one who made better choices.

I intentionally chose to not take the bait Satan often offered me to say cutting remarks, pile on shame, or present myself as the one who made better choices.

Forgiveness is a process. Healing is a long journey. And I'll never, ever criticize another person for choices they made that were different from mine when placed in the same horror and heartbreak as I was. But reconciliation and redemption are not one and the same. Even if your situation doesn't allow for reconciliation, redemption is still yours for the choosing. I experienced redemption with God before my marriage reconciled.

But after time had passed, I realized it was possible to heal together. And I'm so grateful Art and I both did the hard work of putting our marriage back together, together. We have made the choice to let God use our story, as messy as it is, because we know others would drown in their own tears if not for seeing the glimmer of hope in ours.

So, my dear friend, if you find yourself today in a situation where you feel like there's nothing else to give but time, I know that painful ache all too well. But I love this verse at the end of Psalm 6, after David's honest cries about his troubles: *"The Lord has heard my plea; the Lord accepts my prayer"* (v. 9 ESV).

God hears your plea.

God accepts your prayer.

And whether it's redemption or reconciliation or a completely different situation from mine, God will breathe life into shattered pieces of your story and create something new and more beautiful than ever before. In His way. In His timing.

God, thank You for working on my behalf even when I am at the end of my own strength. I trust You to bring beauty from my story even when the pieces of it feel so broken. When the only thing I have left to give is time, show me how to live obediently in the waiting moments. In Jesus' name, amen.

A Letter from Lysa

Dearest reader,

I don't know what hard realities you are facing today, friend. But I want to encourage you with what I do know to be true.

It will all be turned upside down in eternity.

Grief will turn to joy. Heartbreak to shouts of thanksgiving. Crowns of thorns to crowns of gold.

The world says it's over.

God declares not until He says so.

The world says it's final.

God reminds us He always has the final say.

The world says impossible.

God comforts our soul by whispering in Him all things are possible.

The world says give up.

God says look up.

I don't know all the ways my story will go while here on earth. But I know with confidence how my story ends. Jesus wins.

Lysa

28

God's Goodness Isn't Canceled

Let the peace of Christ rule in your hearts, since as members of one body you were called to peace.

Colossians 3:15

In 2020, COVID-19 not only spread across the world at record levels, but it also spread across our daily realities and changed so much for so many. What we saw in the news truly felt like something we'd only see in a Hollywood movie—not real life.

Because of the life-threatening potential of the virus, social distancing and canceled gatherings were required precautions. While all of this was necessary, it was also jarring.

It was like life just slammed on the brakes, and we were all reeling from the whiplash. Certainly, in the grand scheme of things, saving lives is always most important. But it left me with all kinds of emotions to process in the middle of the changes.

One of those emotions was the very real feeling of disappointment. Please know processing our disappointments is not only okay—it's emotionally and spiritually necessary. You're not making light of someone else's serious pain when you process your pain to gain a better perspective.

You're not making light of someone else's serious pain when you process your pain to gain a better perspective.

With that as the anthem playing in the background, I want to recall some of the circumstances that were hard on me and those I love during the time of COVID-19. In just a matter of a few weeks:

I helped a friend navigate her canceled wedding.

My husband had to close the dining room of his restaurant.

Many loved ones lost their source of income as businesses closed and couldn't reopen.

Schools closed and canceled sports, plays, graduations, and other events students had worked toward and looked forward to for years.

Family gatherings were canceled.

People we know and love got sick, and some didn't recover. Loved ones had to try to say goodbye over FaceTime when they got the excruciating news there was nothing more that could be done.

Everything we thought we would be doing in that season looked vastly different than we expected, and the feelings of loss that followed were real. As Christians, how do we set our minds and hearts on things above when we are staring at startling realities? Here are some things I wrote in my journal during the time of COVID-19 that helped me.

1. FRAME THE DISAPPOINTMENT BY REMEMBERING WHAT YOU DO HAVE SO YOU DON'T GET CONSUMED BY WHAT'S BEEN TAKEN.

It's incredibly emotional when you've dreamed and planned and invested in what you thought would be a very normal expectation and then your hope is hijacked.

But remember:

- Being good to other people has not been canceled.
- Learning, growing, and maturing have not been canceled.
- The need to grieve and get counseling has not been canceled.
- Fun has not been canceled.
- Love has not been canceled.

Be honest about what you need. And be ever mindful that though COVID-19 changed a lot, it did not change God. It did not change His character. It did not change His love and care for His people. It did not change His plans to take everything we face and use it to grow

God's goodness is not canceled. Rest in that, rejoice in that, be so very reassured because of that.

us, mature us, and make us ever more prepared for a good future.

This disappointment may be a delay, it may be a distraction, even a devastation for a season. But this is not your final destination. God's goodness is not canceled. Rest in that, rejoice in that, be so very reassured because of that.

2. As you remember who God is, use that to bring some perspective into your disappointment.

- God is a protector. He is protecting you from something you can't see.
- God is a provider. He is providing something if only you'll look for it. Just because His provision is different doesn't mean it's not good.
- God is faithful. No matter what disappointment is taking from you right now, place it in the hands of God.
- Give it to Him as your sacrifice. For whatever we willingly place in the hands of God, He will redeem.

3. Resist the temptation to write out worst-case scenarios.

It can be so easy to let today's disappointments get blown out of proportion and make you expect the absolute worst for tomorrow. I'm challenging myself not to mentally run too far into an unknown future and write a script of worst-case scenarios. Often, what I expect tomorrow to bring will start to play out in my attitude. I think, in some weird way, that if I expect hurt and heartbreak and hardships, this protects me from getting caught off guard. But in reality, when I do this, my negativity pulls me away from trusting God, loving people, and enjoying what today offers. And it sometimes even becomes self-fulfilled prophecies as I trade the good of today for living in fear of tomorrow.

Whatever disappointment you are facing today, now is the time to feed your faith and fuel your healthy perspectives. Make the choice today to *"let the peace of Christ rule in your hearts, since as members of one body you were called to peace"* (Colossians 3:15).

God, today I declare disillusioning disappointments and blinding fear don't get to be the boss of me. I am ruled by the peace of Christ, and I will use His truth to frame all I see. Even when I am walking through hard seasons, help me have the attitude of Christ. In Jesus' name, amen.

29

Why Isn't God Answering My Prayer?

We know that for those who love God all things work together for good, for those who are called according to his purpose.

Romans 8:28 ESV

In 2015, the *New York Times* ran an article called "Googling for God."[1] In this article, author Seth Stephens-Davidowitz started by saying, "It has been a bad decade for God, at least so far." He went on to ask, "What questions do people have when they are questioning God?" The number one question was "Who created God?" The number two question was "Why does God allow suffering?" But it was the third question that slammed into my heart and made me realize the depth at which many of us struggle when we walk through devastating situations: "Why does God hate me?"

I'm not alone in wondering about God's feelings when circumstances beg me to feel betrayed. While I would have never used the word *hate*, seeing it typed out as one of the most commonly asked questions about God shows me just how dark our perspective can get. The most devastating spiritual crisis isn't when we wonder why God isn't doing something. It's when we become utterly convinced He no longer cares. And that's what I hear hiding behind that Google search.

And I shudder to say this, but I think that's what was hiding behind my own disillusionment as well. What makes faith fall apart isn't doubt. It's becoming too certain of the wrong things. Things like: *Forgiveness doesn't matter. It's not worth it. It's not time for that kind of obedience. God isn't moving. What I see is absolute proof that God isn't working.*

That's where I can find myself getting more and more skeptical of God's love, God's provision, God's protection, God's instructions, and God's faithfulness. And most of all, where I start fearing He really has no plan at all, and I'm just truly going to be a victim of circumstances beyond anyone's control.

What makes faith fall apart isn't doubt. It's becoming too certain of the wrong things.

The problem with that thinking is, while it may line up with what my life looks like from my place of pain and confusion, it doesn't line up with truth. And before everything went haywire in my life, I had already put a stake in the ground, proclaiming that God's Word is where I would turn and return to no matter what.

I could resist trusting God and turning to His truth. I could run from it. I could, with bitter resignation, put my Bible on a shelf to collect dust for years. But I wouldn't be able to escape what was already buried deep in my heart.

I knew in this deep-down knowing place that what I was seeing wasn't all that was happening. Past experiences where I have seen God's faithfulness remind me that I don't always see God working in the midst of my hard times.

There are a few times in my life where I've seen dramatic moves by God happen quick enough for me to say, "Wow, look what God is doing!" But most of the time it's thousands of little shifts so slight that the dailiness of His work doesn't register in real time.

> It's hard when we are living in that space where our head knows God can do anything, but our heart is heavy because He's not doing what we are hoping for.

It's hard when we are living in that space where our head knows God can do anything but our heart is heavy because He's not doing what we are hoping for, what we've prayed for, what we've believed for, for a long while. I get it—and I've cried many tears because of it.

So what helps? It helps to know these things:

- God is active even if we can't see His activity. Just because we can't discern or detect what He's doing, doesn't mean He isn't working.

We fix our eyes not on what is seen, but on what is unseen, since what is seen is temporary, but what is unseen is eternal. (2 Corinthians 4:18)

- What may feel like a lack of intervention is not a sign of His lack of affection.

This I call to mind and therefore I have hope: Because of the Lord's great love we are not consumed, for his compassions never fail. They are new every morning; great is your faithfulness. (Lamentations 3:21–23)

- God loves us too much to answer our prayers at any other time than the right time, and in any other way than the right way.

We know that for those who love God all things work together for good, for those who are called according to his purpose. (Romans 8:28 ESV)

Today look for beautiful ways God is showing you assurances

of His love. His deep affection is all around you, friend. Even in the waiting places.

God, I confess it's easy for me to become skeptical when things are not working out the way I had planned. Even when I don't see it . . . even when I don't feel it . . . I will stand on the truth that You are working all things together for good. In Jesus' name, amen.

30

When Our Opinions and Feelings Get Us in Trouble

In those days there was no king in Israel. Everyone did what was right in his own eyes.

Judges 21:25 ESV

A few months ago I was walking with a friend when we passed two huge trees that had fallen during a storm. I stopped and asked the guys clearing the trees why those two in particular hadn't been able to withstand the storm.

An older man who'd been working with trees his whole life explained that the first tree had incredibly shallow roots for such a big tree. Its roots had grown used to getting surface water from the sprinkler system. As a result, the roots didn't dig down deep to get water from below. Shallow roots can keep a big tree alive but not stable during storms.

The second tree looked big and strong on the outside, but inside was hollow. At some point an ant had found a weak spot in the tree and started chewing a tiny tunnel into the tree's center. Soon other ants found their way in as well. Then water got in the opening and softened the wood. Over time the tree rotted away internally.

Just because something looks healthy from the outside doesn't mean there's not a completely different reality on the inside.

Just because something looks healthy from the outside doesn't mean there's not a completely different reality on the inside.

These trees make me think of the condition of God's people at the end of the book of Judges: empty and shallow. The final words of this book provide such a heartbreaking reality check even for us today. Judges 21:25 says, *"In those days there was no king in Israel. Everyone did what was right in his own eyes."* Sadly, the patterns of sin and destruction that felt "right" to them were completely outside what God called right and good.

This is where we discover three things that happen when we follow our opinions and feelings (what's right in our own eyes) rather than the absolute truth of God.

1. We mistake opinions for truth.

Just like the tree with shallow roots, if we aren't digging in deep to seek the source of Living Water for ourselves, we won't have the grounding necessary to stand strong when the world's ways try to pull us down. We must seek and apply God's truth every day, so we aren't easily swayed by opinions that aren't in line with His Word. Shallow seeking will lead to shallow believing—that dangerous place where we will fall for whatever opinions make us comfortable and our lives more convenient.

2. We make feelings our false Holy Spirit.

This is like the big tree that was taken down by some small ants. The little ants are like desires that lead to eventual death: *"Then, after desire has conceived, it gives birth to sin; and sin, when it is full-grown, gives birth to death"* (James 1:15). When we care more about what feels right than what is right, we open ourselves up to the destruction of sin. Feelings are wonderful indicators, reminding us to turn to God and let Him direct our desires with His best provisions. But feelings should never be dictators to get our unmet longings and desires met however we see fit.

When we care more about what feels right than what is right, we open ourselves up to the destruction of sin.

3. We will fall when we try to carry the crushing weight of being our own God.

What happens when the king is absent? There is chaos. The book of Judges shows us this reality one story after another, one judge after another. The people are without leadership and direction, and the result is absolute chaos. It makes me think how different the fate of both of those trees could have been if the tree man had been on the scene years before to help them grow big and strong instead of shallow and susceptible.

We need rescue. We need a king. But not just any king; we need the righteous ruler who will right all wrongs, direct and protect us, and redeem and restore all things. We need King Jesus—the perfect Savior who humbled Himself to take on human form and subjected Himself to the cross for the atonement of sin.

We need a king. But not just any king; . . . We need King Jesus.

We aren't kingless like the people in the time of the judges. We have the assurance of knowing our eternal King. We have absolute truth. We have the gift of the Holy Spirit. And we have perspective from reading in His Word how dangerous it is when people just do what is right in their own eyes.

Let's not be people ruled by our

feelings—who merely look confident and capable on the outside. Let's trust our King. Let's follow our King. Let's live by the truth of His Word and become people with true strength residing within.

Father God, I want to be a woman with deep roots. A woman firmly anchored to Your truth and filled by Your Spirit. I confess today how much I need You to lead me, guide me, and be my King. In Jesus' name, amen.

31

The One We Really Need Today

Jesus declared, "I am the bread of life. Whoever comes to me will never go hungry, and whoever believes in me will never be thirsty."

John 6:35

At times I've looked at prayer requests like Amazon Prime deliveries.

I want to place my request. I want what's delivered to look like what I expected and to arrive in record time. And then I will feel so close to God because He did what I wanted!

I'm not proud of this. I'm challenged by it. Because there's something too human and predictable about that being the way prayer actually works. Then my prayers become orders I place, the answers as cheap as products, and the sender nothing more than a far-removed entity I give little thought to until I need something else.

I want to change this. I want to come to God with my needs, my desires, and my hunger, and recognize that whatever He places before me is His daily bread. When Jesus taught us what to pray each day, His first request was for daily bread. But isn't it true that bread took on many different forms in the Bible? Sometimes it looks like a loaf from the oven (Leviticus 2:4), other times like manna from heaven (Deuteronomy 8:3), or best of all, like Jesus who declared Himself as the bread of life (John 6:35). All three are God's perfect provision. But with our human eyes, we would probably only recognize the loaf of bread as good and most fitting, and what a tragedy that would be.

The loaf of bread may be what I want from God, but isn't the loaf the least miraculous of all the forms of bread? It's the kind of provision we have to work to receive from the ground, harvesting the wheat, processing it, and then baking it—all with our own hands. But maybe that's what I like so much about the loaf of bread. Since I'm working for it, I have a sense of control over it.

Manna represents what God simply gives. The manna that fell from heaven for the children of Israel was God's perfect sustenance, even though it looked more like little seeds or flakes rather than loaves of bread. And yet it came directly from God day by day and kept more than two million Israelites alive in the desert for the forty years they needed it. It was miraculous. But even with manna, people had some part to play. They had to go outside their tents to pick it up. They didn't grow it, but they could count on it.

Control and consistency make me feel like I'm trusting God when, in reality, I'm just counting on Him to the level that He comes through for me.

Control and consistency make me feel like I'm trusting God when, in reality, I'm just counting on Him to the level that He comes through for me.

The best kind of bread, though, is the bread of life: Jesus Himself. This isn't provision we work for or provision we simply pick up; this is provision in Christ deposited inside of us that nourishes and sustains us all the way down to our souls. In John 6:35, *"Jesus declared, 'I am the bread of life. Whoever comes to me will never go hungry, and whoever believes in me will never be thirsty.'"* Jesus is the most miraculous provision, and the one already given to us today—but maybe the one least recognized as being everything we need.

And I know you might be saying, "Look, Lysa, what's in front of me is awful, so this doesn't make me want to trust God more. It makes me trust Him less!" I understand that. I feel the same way about some of what's in front of me right now too.

If we have Jesus today, we are living in answered prayer and provision. The One who brings about good, even from the awful we are seeing with our physical eyes, is actively working on our behalf right now. He is talking to the Father about you in ways that, if you could hear Him, would make you never afraid of what is in front of you. Never question His love for you or His goodness to you.

We see only what the human mind can imagine, but God is building something we cannot even fathom. We may see it in time, or not until eternity. But until we see it, we can know with certainty that whatever He gives us truly is His good provision, whether that good is for today or part of a much bigger plan.

Jesus is the most miraculous provision, and the one already given to us today—but maybe the one least recognized as being everything we need.

So today, friend, we can pray what we need to pray. Pray all the words, let the tears flow into sobs and frustrations mixed with hope. And then we can look at what's right in front of us through what we know to be true about God. And trust Jesus to also make it beautiful.

Jesus, thank You for being the perfect sustenance that I need today. I look to You as the Bread of Life, knowing You take care of all my needs. I know You are always working on my behalf. I trust You. In Jesus' name, amen.

A Letter from Lysa

Dear friend,

You're beautiful. I know you doubt it and deny it and feel quite the opposite some days.

Even so, it's true. Because God's fingerprints dance all inside you. Don't cheapen this reality by only looking for it skin deep.

Beauty emerges from one's soul. It's a choice made within that gets more apparent and appealing with age.

Leave traces of beauty wherever you go. Remember, it's yours to give away through your words, your smile, your creativity, and your generous spirit.

Lysa

32

When Unchangeable Feels Unforgivable

Overcome evil with good.

Romans 12:21

When you think better days are ahead, you say things like, "I dream of one day being a wife and mom, or an actress, or a chef, or a scientist." Or, "I dream of one day opening my own coffee shop or writing a book."

But when you are grieving over something or someone that was taken away, you wish you could go back in time. You dream backward.

Grieving is dreaming in reverse.

Instead of hoping for what will one day be, you long for a more innocent time when you lived more unaware of tragedy. So healing feels impossible, because circumstances feel unchangeable.

Grieving is dreaming in reverse.

See if you resonate with any of these unchangeable situations:

- When someone takes something I will never get back.
- When I have to face not just the end of a relationship but the end of all the dreams and future plans that were attached to this person.
- When the pain seems never-ending.
- When the outcome seems so final I'm not sure how to go on.
- When someone hurts not just me but my whole family.
- When the reminders of the pain never end, because the one who hurt me is family.
- When they ruined an opportunity I'd worked my whole life for.
- When they took the life of someone I loved.
- When they hurt me so deeply and wounded me so gravely, I'll never feel normal again.

With a grief so deep from all these painful situations, it's completely maddening to think forgiveness should apply here. What would forgiveness even accomplish? Why go through the deep work to forgive if it really wouldn't make any kind of a difference? And even if you did decide to forgive, how do you forgive when the ones who hurt you can't or won't be willing to cooperate?

I understand all these questions, because I've asked them

and wrestled through them myself. And while I will be the first in line to raise my hand and admit forgiveness is a hard step to take, it's also the only step that leads to anything good. Every other choice—including the choice not to do anything and remain where we are—just adds more hurt upon hurt. Here are a few truths I've been learning to hang on to in my heart when I'm struggling to step toward forgiveness.

Forgiveness is a hard step to take. It's also the only step that leads to anything good.

1. FORGIVENESS IS MORE SATISFYING THAN REVENGE. (ROMANS 12:19–21)

Revenge is you paying twice for a hurt that someone else did to you. You may think it will make you feel better in the short term, but in the long term it will always cost you more emotionally and spiritually than you'd ever want to pay. The only thing your revenge will do is add your wrongdoing on top of theirs.

Forgiveness doesn't let the other person off the hook. It actually places them in God's hands. And then, as you walk through the forgiveness process, it softens your heart. The peace from forgiveness is more satisfying than revenge.

2. Our God is not a do-nothing God. (1 Peter 5:7)

I was recently participating in a Q&A session where someone in the audience asked, "How can God just do nothing?" The pain in her question was deep. Gracious, do I ever understand what that feels like. I remember feeling so disillusioned during my journey with Art. When you are suffering so much that each next breath seems excruciating, it's easy to start assuming God is doing nothing.

But we don't serve a do-nothing God. He is always working. God is always doing something. God is there in the midst of it all. With Art, God wasn't just trying to change his behavior. He was rescuing his soul. There was never one moment when God was doing nothing.

3. The enemy is the real villain. (Ephesians 6:11–12)

Yes, people do have a choice to sin against us or not. And certainly, when we are hurt, the person hurting us may have willingly played into the enemy's plan. But it helps me to remember that this person isn't my real enemy. The devil is real and on an all-out assault against all things good. He hates the word *together*. And he especially works with great intentionality against anything that brings honor and glory to God.

Oh, friend, the heartbreaks you carry are enormous. And your desire to undo some of what has been done is so very understandable. Honestly, on some levels that's honorable. It's okay to carry both the desire to want things to change and an acceptance that on this side of eternity they won't change. You can carry both. You can honor both.

Adding truth into our perspective makes even the unchangeable forgivable. None of this is simple. These aren't truths to simply read through but to sit with. And sit in. Until we can dare to walk in it. Live it out. And maybe even one day declare it as a truth we've decided to own.

Lord, help me not just make peace with things that are unchangeable but move forward in the beauty of forgiveness. I know You are not a do-nothing God, and I trust You with all the heartbreak I'll face on this side of eternity. In Jesus' name, amen.

33

As Far As It Depends on Me

If possible, so far as it depends on you, live peaceably with all.

Romans 12:18 ESV

There's some interesting context around our key verse today that's worth considering and unpacking.

Paul didn't write what became the book of Romans while on a peaceful vacation with peaceful people and peaceful circumstances. He wrote this instruction in the midst of people opposing him and situations filled with hardship.

One of the reasons he wrote his letter to the Romans is that peace would not have been easy for them. It would have felt as unnatural to them as it does for us in the midst of constant hardships, never-ending opposition, and relational differences.

I relate to this so much. It seems I wake up each day with a new set of issues. Maybe today it isn't a big, heartbreaking, life-changing event that's eroding your peace. Maybe it's an ongoing frustration or disappointment with a neighbor. Or a misunderstanding with someone you thought you could trust or even a rude comment someone made to you at work. Conflicts seem to never end.

Yet Paul was reminding everyone who will read these verses that peace is possible.

The Greeks thought of peace as the absence of hostility. But Paul taught that peace is the atmosphere we can bring into hostility. This peace is a wholeness we have because of our relationship with God.

In John 14:27, Jesus said, *"Peace I leave with you; my peace I give you. I do not give to you as the world gives. Do not let your hearts be troubled and do not be afraid."*

The peace referred to here is "to keep or maintain peace."[2] Peace is a gift that God gives believers, and that gift is evidence to the world that we are different because of our union with Christ. Our union with Christ makes this peace possible.

Peace isn't the absence of hostility. Peace is the atmosphere we can bring into hostility.

But it's our demonstration of this peace, especially in the midst of hardships, that makes this peace recognizable as particularly rare and odd.

To live peaceably with all seems like such a ridiculous impossibility. And yet when the impossible is made possible because of Jesus in us, there's no greater testimony that can be shared.

This kind of peace is rich evidence of the reality of Jesus.

There is nothing more powerful to bring into a situation than the Prince of Peace Himself (Isaiah 9:6). At just the utterance of the name of Jesus, peace is there.

And don't miss the context of all of this. Paul didn't say, "As far as it depends on other people bringing peace." Nor did he say, "As long as the conflicts end in a peaceful way. " No, he said, "So far as it depends on *you*."

In other words, peace in my life isn't being prevented by other people's choices. It's made possible by *my choices.*

And that's when I admit I just want to lie down on the floor and loudly declare, "*But I am not Jesus!*" Ugh.

Friend, this truly is possible.

So, while this teaching can feel challenging, it's also eye-opening and empowering. I always thought peace was possible when there was an absence of chaos. But chaos comes and goes as it pleases in this sin-soaked world. I can't control the chaos. But I can control my choices.

Now I'm realizing the antithesis of peace isn't chaos. It's selfishness. And the very best way for me to uninvite selfishness is in the humility of forgiveness.

Peace is the evidence of a life of forgiveness.

Peace is the evidence of a life of forgiveness.

It's not that the people all around you are peaceful, or that all of your relationships are perfectly peaceful all the time. Rather, it's having a deep-down knowing that you've released yourself from the binding effects and constricting force of unforgiveness and the constraining feelings of unfairness.

You've traded all that drama for an upgrade: peace.

Living in the comfort of peace is so much better than living in the constraints of unforgiveness.

This makes such a difference in my life. It's part of my process of cooperating with God. Overcoming evil with good. Living at peace so long as it depends on me.

Leaving room for God to work on the one I need to forgive. Praying for the mercy of God. Seeking the face of God. Knowing the goodness of God. Living in the presence of God.

And in that, I'm seeing the beauty of God.

Jesus, today I pray that You show me how to be a peacemaker and a peacekeeper. As the Prince of Peace, steady my heart to surrender control of situations over to You. I open myself up today to be used by You as an instrument of peace, so give me the courage to live boldly and fight against my flesh in the process. In Jesus' name, amen.

34

Suspicious of God

My heart is steadfast, O God, my heart is steadfast! I will sing and make melody!

Psalm 57:7 ESV

I trust God. Until I don't. That doesn't feel like a very Christian thing to say. But if I don't acknowledge this struggle, I can't address it.

I don't think I'm the only one.

So many of us are standing in our churches on Sunday morning with our hands raised high as we proclaim our God is a "good, good Father," but then we find ourselves lying in our beds on Sunday night with tear-stained pillows, facing realities that don't feel very good at all.

It's hard not to feel suspicious of God when our circumstances don't seem to line up with His promises. And it's difficult not to doubt the light of His truth when everything around us looks dark.

Which brings us to Psalm 57—a passage penned by David in the midst of a season when his circumstances and God's promises appeared to be in complete and total opposition.

At this point David had already been anointed as the future king of Israel (1 Samuel 16:1–13) and had faithfully served King Saul. Sadly, though, Saul "rewarded" David for his service and obedience with persecution and death threats. David was left to run for his life and then hide out in a cave.

When I was in Israel, I had a guide show me a cave that may have been the exact one David hid in during this period of his life. It isn't like the caves I picture in my mind. The entrance looks like a hole in the ground. And as you descend into it, the darkness is overwhelming. As I sat deep down in this cave I pictured David, afraid of going out because of Saul's death threats but also afraid of staying inside this place of unknown darkness.

Scripture also reveals David wasn't hiding alone. This anointed but not-yet-appointed king was leading a pretty discouraging group of men. First Samuel 22:1–2 describes these four hundred men as in distress, in debt, and discontented. Not exactly the positive, resourceful, and hopeful type of people you want to have with you during one of the darkest seasons of your life.

I wouldn't judge David for one second if he had cried out to God in total frustration, saying, "I don't understand any of this. I'm leading a bunch of unsettled and unstable people. We are hiding in a cave. And I'm feeling utterly defeated and completely hopeless!"

But the words he wrote in Psalm 57 are neither exclusively a psalm of lament nor a psalm of thanksgiving. David didn't deny the darkness of his situation, but he also refused to allow his soul to get stuck in a place of despair. Instead, David chose to declare praises about the true nature and character of God. He reminded his soul of who God is—a God who fulfills His purposes (v. 2), a God who saves (v. 3), a God known for His faithfulness and steadfast love (vv. 2, 10).

Even though David's soul was *"bowed down"* by his circumstances (v. 6), he allowed what he knew to be true about God to steady him. This enabled David to declare in our key verse today: *"My heart is steadfast, O God, my heart is steadfast! I will sing and make melody!"* (v. 7 ESV).

I love knowing the story behind this psalm. In a cave that surely felt like an end to all he hoped and dreamed, David acknowledged his distress, but he also lifted his eyes to praise God. David's praise wasn't in vain. It steadied his heart. And his painful circumstances weren't wasted. God used those hardships to mature David. Yes, David had already been anointed to eventually become king. But it was in the womb of the earth where God met him and birthed in him a heart ready to lead.

Praise may not shift our circumstances, but it will definitely begin to change our hearts.

Darkness was the perfect training ground for David's destiny. And those difficult places we so desperately want to be done with can become good training ground for us as well. But we have some choices to make. Will we see this dark time as a womb or a tomb? Is it a birth of something new or the death of what we thought should be? Will we fix our eyes on the truth of God's goodness, or will we give in to hopelessness and despair?

Oh, friend. I know the dark places are scary. But let's choose to believe there is purpose in every season, even the ones that don't seem to make any sense. Let's ask God to birth something new inside of us, allowing Him to do a work in us that will better prepare us to walk out His promises. And instead of being suspicious of Him, let's lift up our praises to Him.

Praise may not shift our circumstances, but it will definitely begin to change our hearts. We don't always get to choose our situations, but we can choose how we live through them.

Father God, thank You so much for reminding me that I am never forsaken or forgotten. You see me in this dark place, and You promise there is purpose here. Bring Your life and light where all hope seems lost, Lord. Show me how to live authentically today, making room for both sorrow and praise to coexist together. In Jesus' name, amen.

35

Brushstrokes of Compassion

As God's chosen people, holy and dearly loved, clothe yourselves with compassion, kindness, humility, gentleness and patience.

Colossians 3:12

Painting was the last thing I expected to be doing on my forty-eighth birthday. And yet there I was, holding a dripping paintbrush beside my mom and my sisters.

Year forty-eight was supposed to be a year filled with adventure and freedom. The last of my five kids was going to college, and Art and I were heading into our empty-nest years. I thought this new season would be as fun and predictable as one of those beautiful adult coloring books. The picture is already perfectly drawn, so all you have to do is follow along and add color.

But nothing looked like I thought it would on this birthday. Instead of planning for the future with my husband, I was trying to figure out how we'd ever glue the shattered pieces of our marriage back together again. Instead of dreaming, I felt like I was stuck in a nightmare. One where I opened the coloring book, and someone had erased all the beautifully drawn lines.

There was nothing but white pages. Empty spaces. Endless possibilities of fear and failure.

Metaphorically speaking, my life was now a blank canvas.

And so my mother suggested—no, actually she demanded—we get some blank canvases and paint on my birthday.

I painted a boat. They all painted angels. And while my mom was right—it was therapeutic in many ways—it was also a terrifyingly vulnerable experience.

The enemy of my soul didn't want me painting that day. To create meant I would look a little bit like my Creator. To overcome the terrifying angst of the blank canvas meant I would forever have more compassion for other artists. You'd better believe as I placed the first blue and gray strokes onto the white emptiness before me, "not good enough" was pulsing through my head in almost deafening tones.

Perfection mocked my boat. The bow was too high, the details too elementary, the reflection on the water too abrupt, and the back of the boat too off-center. Disappointment demanded I hyper-focus on what didn't look quite right.

I forced myself to send a picture of my boat to at least twenty friends. With each text I sent, I slowly made peace with my painting's imperfections. Not for validation but rather confirmation that I could see the imperfections in my painting but not deem it worthless. I could see the imperfections in me and not deem myself worthless. It was an act of self-compassion.

We must get to this place of self-compassion if we ever hope to have true, deep compassion for others. Disappointment begs us to be secretly disgusted with everything and everyone who has gaps, everything and everyone who also wrestles with the "not good enough" script. But what if, instead of being so epically disappointed with everyone, we saw in them the need for compassion?

I like that word, *compassion*. Compassion is being aware that all of us fear the imperfections deeply carved into our naked selves. We all cover up. And then we all get stripped bare when the wins become losses.

And who do we want standing near us in those moments dripping with disappointment and saturated with sorrow? It's those clothed with garments of understanding. They have personally experienced how excruciatingly painful it can sometimes be to simply be human. They keep in mind Colossians 3:12, *"As God's chosen people, holy and dearly loved,*

> Compassion is being aware that all of us fear the imperfections deeply carved into our naked selves.

clothe yourselves with compassion, kindness, humility, gentleness and patience."

We are to put on each of these every day, like a painter puts on her canvas a color she knows will connect her creation with others. God wants us, His creation, to connect with others and bring them light and life with the brushstrokes of compassion.

Have you walked through an unexpected season of darkness and suffering? Those seasons aren't for nothing, my friend. We find life-giving purpose and meaning when we allow God to take our painful experiences and comfort others.

Pick up the paintbrush. Put some paint on the emptiness. Color-correct your perspective. Forget the cravings for comfort zones. Trade your judgment for compassion. Put the brush to the canvas. Declare yourself a painter. And when someone steals all the lines from your coloring book, determine to color the world anyway with the same generous love God offers every day.

You are walking the way of the artist. And I love you for that. I love whatever is about to come to life on your canvas to the glory of our Almighty Creator. God. The Redeemer of dust. The Redeemer of us. Never is a life more beautiful than when you declare it beautiful.

Never is a life more beautiful than when you declare it beautiful.

Father God, no matter how much this life leaves me hurting, I always want to come out on the other side of pain loving. Help me be a woman of great compassion. A woman who wears her scars of suffering well—sharing my survival story so others can know and believe survival is possible for them too. In Jesus' name, amen.

A Letter from Lysa

Dear friend,

Knowing why something happened will never help if we wouldn't agree with the answer anyhow. Seeking answers is understandable. I want to know why too.

But it's so much more comforting to invite God's peace to just fill in the gaps of all the unknowns.

It's when we decide to stop the relentless grasping for unanswerable questions that our hands are then free to take hold of what He has for us next.

God doesn't want to be explained away. He wants to be invited in.

Lysa

36

About My Anger

"In your anger do not sin": Do not let the sun go down while you are still angry, and do not give the devil a foothold.

Ephesians 4:26–27

I used to misunderstand today's key verses and use them in the completely wrong way. It was so convenient to pull them out when someone wanted to go to bed and I still wanted to talk about whatever was causing a conflict.

"Oh, no, you can't call timeout right now. We have to keep talking about this because the Bible says, 'Do not let the sun go down on your anger.' Clearly, the sun is going down, so we have to resolve this."

The first three words in today's key verse, *"in your anger,"* are what I've been missing. It doesn't say, "In *their* anger they better not sin. They better not let the sun go down while *we* are still processing."

When we read Scripture, we have to make sure we're reading it for what it actually says, and not reading it for what we want it to say.

So when I read these verses for what they really say, I realize it's not so much about resolving all relational issues before 9:00 p.m. It's talking about *my* anger, not our frustration.

When we read Scripture, we have to make sure we're reading it for what it actually says, and not reading it for what we want it to say.

As I look more into this passage, it's like the writer of Ephesians, Paul, was saying, "You've got to deal with this anger. Don't lie in your bed and let it consume your mind. If it does, it will come out of your mouth and reveal who or what is mastering you."

Whenever I study Scripture, I challenge myself to go back to the very first time a word or topic is mentioned. I did this with the word *anger* and found myself in Genesis 4 where we encounter the first relational conflict in Scripture. Starting in verse 2 we read about Adam and Eve's children, brothers named Cain and Abel.

> *Now Abel kept flocks, and Cain worked the soil. In the course of time Cain brought some of the fruits of the soil as an offering to the* Lord. *And Abel also brought an offering—fat portions from some of the first-born of his flock. The* Lord *looked with favor on Abel and his offering,*

> *but on Cain and his offering he did not look with favor. So Cain was very angry, and his face was downcast.*
>
> *Then the Lord said to Cain, "Why are you angry? Why is your face downcast? If you do what is right, will you not be accepted? But if you do not do what is right, sin is crouching at your door; it desires to have you, but you must rule over it." Now Cain said to his brother Abel, "Let's go out to the field." While they were in the field, Cain attacked his brother Abel and killed him.* (Genesis 4:2–8)

I've known the story of these two brothers for years, but I missed a really important detail. In between Cain getting angry and killing his brother, the Lord came and talked with him. The Lord Himself said to Cain, "Why are you angry? Why are you doing that? Why are you letting your anger consume so much of you? Why is your face downcast?"

And suddenly it's not so much a story about Cain and Abel; God is speaking to me.

And I'm blown away by this pattern God revealed to me in Scripture: what we let consume our *mind* makes its way out through our *mouth*, revealing the real source of what's driving our decisions. Are we relying on our ever-changing desires, emotions, and frustrations to help us navigate what we are facing? Or are we relying on Jesus' truth that can set us free? We must always remember that we can acknowledge our feelings, tend to what needs to be addressed because of our feelings, but not be ruled by our feelings.

I see it here in the story of Cain and Abel:

1. **His mind**: Cain refused to humble himself and allowed this anger to fester inside him.
2. **His mouth**: Cain was not willing to let forgiveness spill from his lips.
3. **What ruled him**: The sin that was crouching at his door deeply ruled over him, so much that he killed his brother. He gave his feelings the right to dictate his actions, even after God came and talked with him.

I saw the same word for *anger* in Ephesians 4:26–27, 1 Peter 5:6–9, and James 4:7–11, if you want to look up the verses. And as I continued to read through Scripture, I became aware that I must get intentional when I go to bed every night.

I must not let anger and frustration run rampant through my thoughts.

But sometimes it's hard, because the hurt is so fresh or the frustration is so ongoing. Those are the times I don't know what to do with myself, when I'm lying in my bed and I have unresolved feelings that just won't go away on their own.

But isn't God so gracious that He gives us today's key verse and ties this valuable lesson to something we all get to see every night? As the sun is going down, I pray that we remember it's time to pause and let God tend to any strong or potentially damaging reactions to hurts that could consume us.

Not letting our emotions consume us does not negate the conflict we're experiencing or our need to address things tomorrow. It's about tending to our heart so anger doesn't turn into bitterness. The human heart has such a propensity to turn festering hurt into hate. And that's why the Lord instructed Cain to rule over the sin and not let it master him. The best way I know to do that in those moments when I can literally feel the anger begging me to say or do things that completely betray my true heart is to say, "Father, I need Your forgiveness to flow to me and through me right now so Your Spirit can work in me and sweep my heart clean." This doesn't make light of or deny my hurt; it puts it in the hands of God so He can help me better process it.

Forgiveness is a complicated grace that uncomplicates my anger and helps me see beautiful again.

Forgiveness is a complicated grace that uncomplicates my anger and helps me see beautiful again.

Don't read past that statement too quickly. Remember, our ability to forgive others rises and falls on whether we lean into what Jesus has already done. I must receive His grace for me and then allow that same grace to freely flow through me to others.

This is the Spirit of God working in us. And where the Spirit is, good can be worked. Peace can be found. Healing words can be spoken. Balled-up fists can be released. Gentler answers can be given. Progress can be made. The enemy can be defeated. God can be glorified. And the watching world can see more and more of the reality of Jesus in us.

Jesus, remind me when the sun sets each day that it is time to sweep my heart clean of any lingering anger and unforgiveness. Thank You for the forgiveness You have extended to me. Use me as an instrument of forgiveness today. In Jesus' name, amen.

37

The Daily Cure for a Heavy Heart

"This, then, is how you should pray . . ."

Matthew 6:9

In the previous devotion, we talked about keeping our hearts swept clean so Jesus can use us as an instrument of forgiveness to others.

I want to show you one more passage of Scripture today that teaches us how to really do this.

In Matthew 6, we read Jesus teaching the disciples how to pray, more commonly known as the Lord's Prayer. There's so much He could teach us to include in our daily prayers, right? I mean, if I were tasked with the job of teaching how to pray, I'm afraid I may have included all the wrong things and left out some really important things.

And you know what I may have been tempted to minimize or exclude? The very parts Jesus seems to emphasize the most—confession and forgiveness.

In Matthew 6:9–13, Jesus taught:

This, then, is how you should pray:

"Our Father in heaven,
hallowed be your name,
your kingdom come,
your will be done,
on earth as it is in heaven.
Give us today our daily bread.
And forgive us our debts,
as we also have forgiven our debtors.
And lead us not into temptation,
but deliver us from the evil one."

And then in the next two verses right after the Lord's Prayer, Jesus added, *"For if you forgive other people when they sin against you, your heavenly Father will also forgive you. But if you do not forgive others their sins, your Father will not forgive your sins"* (vv. 14–15).

The importance of receiving and giving forgiveness makes up most of the prayer. If you look at the word count of this teaching of Jesus in the New International Version in the Bible, the total teaching is ninety-four words. The topic of giving and receiving forgiveness takes up forty-six of those words. Wow.

This grabs my attention and makes me want to lean in a little more to what Jesus wanted us to do on a daily basis besides just making our prayers about requesting help and provision from God.

The Lord's Prayer reminds us what the human heart needs every day—we need God, we need to be forgiven, and we need to forgive. Which means forgiveness is supposed to be as much a part of our daily lives as eating and sleeping.

The Lord's Prayer reminds us what the human heart needs every day—we need God, we need to be forgiven, and we need to forgive.

But I will readily admit, I'm not even sure I've ever done this weekly, much less daily. And maybe that's the very reason I often have an unexplainable heavy feeling inside of me.

We live in a day and time when being offended almost seems to go hand in hand with being alive. Almost everyone is epically offended by something. Almost everyone has relationship troubles. And I would guess almost none of us are truly praying daily with confession and forgiveness like Jesus taught us.

I'll be the first in line to raise my hand and admit this is me. I'm too easily offended. I'm too slow to turn to prayer. I'm very rarely confessing. And I'm too often not forgiving.

But I want to change this. I want to mature in this.

And remember, feeling angry is different from living angry. Feeling offended is different from living offended. Feeling skeptical is different from living skeptical. Feeling wronged is different from living wronged. Feeling resentment is different from living resentful. Jesus knew we'd have all these feelings, especially when there's so much unpredictability in our circumstances, our relationships, and even our own emotions. So Jesus gives us a prayer to pray each day that helps us get ahead of all we'll face today with confession and forgiveness.

I know I won't do this perfectly. But that doesn't mean I don't try it at all.

Just a few weeks ago, someone I've been trying to help completely blindsided me with a reaction that felt extremely out of character and honestly undeserved. I was hurt. All I wanted to do was pull back from helping and give way to a full unleashing of my hurt on her. I could feel bitterness rising up.

But instead of immediately reacting, I remembered how earlier that morning I had prayed the Lord's Prayer and confessed several things to the Lord in which my own heart needed some work.

I'd pre-decided to forgive those who might do or say something that might hurt me or stir up my strong emotion that day.

Instead of letting my anger stir me to cause more hurt and pain, I simply let my anger inform me that something needed to be settled between my friend and me. I asked her if she could come over to my house and instead of us trying to figure it out or talk it out, maybe we could pray it through together.

Confession breaks the cycle of chaos inside of me.

Forgiveness breaks the cycle of chaos between us.

I let the Jesus in me talk to the Jesus in her. I let the Jesus in her talk to the Jesus in me. As we prayed, the most unexplainable peace washed over us both. It didn't necessarily solve the issue at hand. But it did prevent the chaos of adding in more hurt, more confusion, and more opportunities for resentment.

The Lord's Prayer prepared my heart for something I didn't even know was coming later that day.

The best time to forgive is before we are ever offended.

The next best time to forgive is right now.

Jesus, thank You for teaching me how to pray—not necessarily the prayer I want to pray sometimes, but the prayer I need to pray. Help me remember today that confession and forgiveness are good for my heart, that they help lessen the chaos and lift the heaviness I sometimes feel deep inside. In Jesus' name, amen.

38

More Than Dust and Bone

And God saw everything that he had made, and behold, it was very good. And there was evening and there was morning, the sixth day.

Genesis 1:31 ESV

Remember who you are.

These are words I spoke to my children countless times when they were younger. I wanted them to remember they are children of the almighty God. I knew if they remembered this truth, they would be better able to live this truth.

Genesis 1 and 2 read like this kind of reminder to me. A reminder I needed when my heart was broken and I could feel everything good slipping away from me. I felt so insignificant. I was trying to move forward after the deep pain of betrayal. I kept asking, "Is it even possible to heal from something like this?" As we navigate a world full of hurt and hearts so often full of shame, these first two chapters of the Bible feel like God whispering to us, "Remember who you are. Remember how I designed you. Remember all I've called you to be."

When God formed and shaped this world and its creatures into being, His goodness seeped in with every thought and touch. And when He was done, Genesis 1:31 ESV says that *"God saw everything that he had made, and behold, it was very good."*

I love that God declared Adam and Eve to be exceedingly and abundantly good, even though the actual ingredients He used to make them were seemingly so very humble and basic. Dust and broken-off bone don't seem like the most promising of beginnings.

Left on their own, these ingredients would amount to nothing. Insignificant. Unacceptable.

But chosen by God and then breathed on and touched by God, they became the only part of creation made in the image of God. They were "nothing" turned into the most glorious "something." They were made to be a reflection of the image of God. These image bearers made an invisible God's image visible.

And I don't want us to miss the significance of Genesis 2:18 when God said He would make a helper suitable for Adam.

The Hebrew word for suitable is דֶגֶנ, *neged*, meaning "what is in front of you, in your sight, before your face in your view." So this word *suitable* gives meaning to the kind of help Adam needed. Beyond just needing help to work the garden or needing someone uniquely designed to be able to carry children so they could bring forth life, Adam needed a visual—something in front of him to view. This seems to me to be a reflection. Not like a mirror reflecting only what you place in front of it. No, this was more like a reminder that what was standing in front of him was a reflection of God's image.

It seems Eve, in being a helper suitable for him, was to be a reminder of who Adam was—a human made in God's image. A reflection of the glory of God and goodness of God. It was a reminder Eve would have needed as well. And together they were to fill the earth with the glory of God. Not just to be fruitful and multiply it with children. But to multiply evidence of God Himself (Genesis 1:28).

Their design in the image of God declared to the world, "God is worthy of praise!"

And their design declared to each other, "Remember who you are. You are of God. From God. Made in His image. Loved from the depth of God's unfathomable Father's heart. Treasured beyond imagination."

Remember who you are. You are of God. From God. Made in His Image.

This is the Divine Echo. This is what Adam and Eve were called to, and it's what we're called to as well. Not just married people, but every person with a beating heart. And the more we remind each other of who we really are, the more God's goodness and glory will echo throughout the earth.

We aren't just dust and bone.

We aren't what we've done or what's been done to us.

We aren't the worst of what others have said about us.

We are the very breath and touch of God. Designed and loved by God. A reflection of the glory and goodness of God.

These are the truths I needed to remember about who I am. I am so much more than the sum total of my hurt and pain and insecurities. Maybe it's what you need as well . . . so let me whisper to your soul, "Remember who you are."

Father God, what a humbling and beautiful gift it is to be Your image bearer. Help me to change how I see myself and others. Show me if there's anyone I've been viewing through a lens of hurt and shame instead of Your divine lens of love. I want my life to be a declaration of Your goodness and glory. And I want to speak life and truth into hurting hearts who have forgotten who they are. In Jesus' name, amen.

39

When Your Husband Has Given Up

For you formed my inward parts; you knitted me together in my mother's womb. I praise you, for I am fearfully and wonderfully made. Wonderful are your works; my soul knows it very well.

Psalm 139:13–14 ESV

I know the heart-ripping hopelessness of a relationship unraveling.

The silence. The rejection. The harsh words. The absence of intimacy. The questions. The lack of answers. The hurt.

In the early days and months that followed the shattering discovery of my husband's affair, I remember wishing I could be put to sleep like when you have surgery. Why is it they only call in the anesthesiologists when you are surgically cut open? When you are being ripped open emotionally, it's no less painful.

The shock and heartbreak and relationship implosion impacted every level of my life. Nothing was left untouched or undamaged. And I felt the harsh realities every single day.

Days turned into months. Months turned into years. And slowly I turned into someone I didn't recognize. My strong but normally carefree spirit became a confusing mix of anxiety, panic attacks, and soul-blinding pain so intense I thought I'd never feel healthy or regain a sense of normalcy again. And because I'd been through so much that was so hard to process, a darkness started to cloud my outlook that used to be so optimistic.

I'm forever grateful my marriage has been reconciled. But that doesn't mean the road of healing from something so heartbreaking has been easy or that the journey hasn't felt painfully long.

This is why my heart aches for anyone in a marriage that's struggling.

And I think one of the deepest hurts comes when one spouse resigns while the other is still trying. There is a panic that arises to somehow make the other person wake up, stop their resignation, and stop all the destruction.

A situation like this is much more complicated than simple answers I could offer here. And whether you're married or not, I want to give you one stepping stone upon which to stand today in whatever situation you feel panicked in:

Decide today that you are worthy.

Because you are. Worthy. You may not feel like it. But a quick glimpse at Psalm 139 assures me that you are. You are *fearfully and wonderfully made* by a loving God who cares for you. Who loves you. And I'd rather depend on the solid truth of God than the roller coaster of fickle feelings.

You are beautiful and captivating and smart and capable. But if you are in a relationship full of unmet expectations, unresolved issues, and frustrating communication, I suspect you feel a little less than all I've described.

Broken-down relationships can really break down a woman.

And if you're anything like me, when you feel broken down, those around you get your worst. Then upon all the hurt and anxiety, you layer regret, shame, and the feeling that you've lost yourself. You've lost that girl inside who used to be so positive and happy and ready to take on the world.

Decide today that you are worthy. Because you are.

Can I whisper a tender truth to you? The only way to recapture her is to come up for air and remember: *You are worthy because the Creator of the universe says you are.*

Then you can act worthy.

And step aside from the emotional yuck to make some level-headed decisions. Get a plan. Talk to wise people who love you, provide godly counsel, and will walk this tough journey with you.

Draw some healthy and helpful boundaries with your husband, if some are needed.

Pray like crazy for clear discernment. Because Jesus is the best source of help.

Honest cries for help, lifted up to Jesus, will not go unheard. He sees. He knows. He loves. And Jesus will direct you as long as you stick with Him.

Remember, you can't control how others act and react, but you can control how you act and react.

I pray your relationship survives. I pray it with every fiber of my being. But if it doesn't, I pray most of all that the beautiful woman you are rises above all that fell apart, still clinging tightly to the only opinion that matters—the One who forever calls you worthy.[3]

Dear Lord, when my marriage is struggling, I feel so consumed with pain and fear. Help me please. I need to hold on to Your truths that I am worthy. And God, please show me the wise and healing steps I can take right now. In Jesus' name, amen.

A Letter from Lysa

Dear friend,

This is what I want to declare over you as you keep processing challenging relationship situations: Don't let unforgiveness weigh you down. You deserve to stop suffering because of what other people have done to you.

So make today the day you start to let go of all the frustrations, resentments, and grudges.

You don't need to edit your words for God. You just need to pour it all out. Open the case files and examine the proof. Not to use against others but to see it all in light of God's truth. Let Him reveal what you need to learn from all this and take the lessons with you, but don't weaponize your pain against others.

That collected proof is not a treasure, nor is it a

souvenir proving the hard place you've traveled to, or your secret weapon of justice. It's debris. Though you believe it's protecting you and making your world better, it's not healing your heart.

I'm so sorry for how they hurt you. And I don't know why they did what they did or left when they left. I'm guessing they thought you better off without them or didn't think of you at all. They couldn't see you like you needed or love you like you pleaded. They just had to go. But answers about why are not what you need. Waiting for something from them holds you hostage to what the other person might not ever be willing to give.

When we let the hurt go and the grudges leave, perspective—a really great gift—is what we'll receive. Perspective will bring a sense of revival, and an assurance of survival in your heart and mind. Don't give up; don't give in; don't get lost along the way. Persevere by pressing in and finally letting the proof go.

Your heart will feel lighter, your mood so much brighter, and life can now go on.

40

Five Things to Say to a Friend Today

Be joyful in hope, patient in affliction, faithful in prayer. Share with the Lord's people who are in need. Practice hospitality.

Romans 12:12–13

I remember sitting in the smelly middle school gym like it was yesterday.

I'd survived the awkward and much-dreaded moments of changing into my PE uniform in the girls' locker room. And now I sat on the hard bleachers listening to the squeak of tennis shoes, the uneven cadence of bouncing balls, the teacher's sharp whistle, and the girls laughing behind me.

They weren't laughing "with" me. That would have meant I was accepted, wanted, and invited in to be a part of their group.

No, they were laughing "at" me.

I was the subject of their gossip. I was the punchline of their jokes. And it hurt.

I imagine you know that hurt too. Change the scenery and people, and this same hurt can be found in most of our lives:

- When your coworkers all make plans to go to lunch, but you weren't invited.
- When that other preschool mom says, "Several of us moms are concerned with how aggressive your child seems on the playground."
- When everyone else's social media makes marriage look dreamy and uber-romantic as you're crying yourself to sleep.

But on the other hand, there are also those beautiful moments when a friend steps in with a gentle smile and a few simple words of encouragement, and suddenly you're not alone.

I want to be that friend for you today. Through this devotional, we've spent a lot of time diving into our stories so we can move forward as healthy and whole people. But there's another step. We can use our healing perspectives to create healing opportunities for others.

Can I challenge you with what I believe are the five best things one can say to a friend? And then might you give the gift of saying these things to a friend today?

This list is from our key verses, Romans 12:12–13.

1. "YOU'RE WONDERFUL."

(Romans 12:12: *"Be joyful in hope."*)

The world is quick to tell us all the ways we fall short. We are hyper-aware of our faults and frailties. So what a precious gift to remind a friend of specific ways she's a wonderful friend, a wonderful mom, a wonderful wife, a wonderful coworker, a wonderful person. This will be more than just a compliment. This is helping infuse a little joy into her hope.

2. "Me too."

(Romans 12:12: "*patient in affliction*")

What a blessing to remind a friend we all have afflictions, hurts, faults, and tender places. We all get sick both emotionally and physically.

The patient friend freely gives grace because she so desperately needs it herself. "Me too" acknowledges I'm no better than you, but together we are stronger. It's such a loving and disarming admission that we're all in this together.

3. "I'll pray."

(Romans 12:12: "*faithful in prayer*")

Wouldn't it be wonderful to tell a friend every time you see a specific color, object, or number, you'll use it as a reminder to pray for her? And when you do, shoot her a quick text letting her know.

4. "I'll share."

(Romans 12:13: *"Share with the Lord's people who are in need."*)

When we notice a need in a friend's life, might we be willing to step in and be part of the solution?

Recently, I had a friend whose wedding plans to elope were canceled due to COVID-19. My family pulled our resources together and had a small wedding planned for them in eight hours. It wasn't the perfect day they envisioned, but we showed up for them in the best way we could to make their day beautiful. And us just simply seeing the need, and sharing what we had to make her day special, made the sweetest memories for her. She even later wrote in a post on her social media, "It was the most magical day."

5. "Come over."

(Romans 12:13: *"Practice hospitality."*)

Welcoming a friend inside the sacred space of our home is such a needed gesture. There's just something about relationships

As we purposefully ease the loneliness ache in others, we will see it is beautifully eased in us.

that are less pixelated when we get eye to eye, voice to voice, and talk. Really talk.

Over broken bread we share broken hearts. And then we celebrate the parts of us that are still intact. We reach across the table and across our differences to grab hold of the glorious bond of friendship.

I've found as we purposefully ease the loneliness ache in others, we will see it is beautifully eased in us.

Dear Lord, thank You for the gift of friendship I have with the women I get to do life with. I pray today that You would show me how to uplift, encourage, and meet a need in those around me in my community. Put someone on my heart today who needs a touch of love and encouragement. In Jesus' name, amen.

41

Let Bitterness Be a Seed of Potential, Not a Root of Regret

Watch out that no poisonous root of bitterness grows up to trouble you, corrupting many.

Hebrews 12:15 NLT

However loss encounters our life, it hurts.

We have all lost people we once hugged and held and allowed a kind of merging of us with them. And whether they walked away, moved away, drifted away, shoved away, faded away, or passed away, the away-ness created a phantom feeling where, out of habit, we reach for them but they're no longer there.

We dial their number to no avail. We run our fingers across photographs but cannot feel the warmth of their skin. The loss of inside jokes and shared late-night whispers and conflicts and carpools and cookouts and differing opinions and all the other million little daily ways "together" is made. The story of our lives included us both. And now it doesn't.

Loss is also evidence that there was once something there,

even though it's not there now. And as painful as sitting in fresh loss and grief can be, it can also be a good cure for bitterness.

Don't read that last sentence too quickly or your brain may transpose the words to read, "Sitting in fresh grief can be the *cause* of bitterness." While this is true, sometimes how you got into a dark cave is actually the solution to finding your way out.

If loss was the way bitterness got in, maybe revisiting grief will help provide a way out.

First, let me state the obvious that this seems strange, because loss and the resulting grief are often the cause of bitterness. I get that. When your personal loss came because of another person's foolishness, selfishness, meanness, or irresponsibility, sorrow can quickly invite bitterness you didn't even know you were capable of.

Sorrow can quickly invite bitterness you didn't even know you were capable of.

But instead of being just an invited visitor, bitterness moves right into your emptiness without permission. At the time you may not have even realized it or recognized what it was, because, at first, bitter feelings can feel quite justifiable and oddly helpful.

Over time, bitterness doesn't just want to be something that awakens some feeling. It wants to become your only feeling. Bitterness doesn't just want to room with you; it wants to completely consume everything about you. Hebrews 12:15 warns us to *"watch out that no poisonous root of bitterness grows up to trouble you, corrupting many"* (NLT).

You see, bitterness wears the disguises of other chaotic emotions that are harder to attribute to the original source of hurt.

There isn't an ounce of desire in my heart to evoke any kind of condemnation or throw any sort of guilt in your direction. I'm too busy managing my own emotions around this. But what I am saying in the safety of these pages, without any kind of spotlight thrown on you, is this: just consider where bitterness might have moved into some kind of loss or emptiness in your life.

Bitterness doesn't have a core of hate but rather a core of hurt. This isn't a justification of bitterness but rather an observation that can help us not feel not so defensive. When bitter feelings emerge, they're usually tied to deep complexities of being hurt in deep ways, unfair ways, ways that changed so much about life it's almost inconceivable to believe that forgiveness is appropriate.

Bitterness isn't usually found in those whose hearts are hard but rather in those who are most tender. It's not that they are cold; it's that they've been made to feel unsafe. This is a caring person who trusted someone or some people they should have been able to trust. And they were made to feel like a fool when the trust they gave as a gift was trampled and shattered. The sharp edges left behind from broken trust cut them to their core, and the resistance they now demonstrate toward other people is often pure fear of being hurt again. Hardness is often the exact opposite of the way their heart was made to operate, but it's the only way they know to protect themselves.

Bitterness isn't an indication of limited potential in relationships. Usually the bitter heart is the heart with the greatest ability to love deeply. But when you love deeply, you are at the greatest risk of being hurt deeply. And when that deep hurt comes, it seems to cage the love that once ran wild and free. Caged love often has a bitter cry.

Caged love often has a bitter cry.

Being bitter shouldn't be equated to being a bad person. It's most often a sign that a person with great potential for good filled the emptiness of their losses with feelings that are natural but not helpful in times of grief.

Now let me ask you a question: *What is bitterness to you?*

A feeling?

A hard heart?

Evidence of unprocessed grief?

Statements made that hurt because you've been hurt?

Maybe bitterness is a combination of all that and more. We will talk more about what to do with our bitterness in the next devotion. But today I want to give you one more possibility for what bitterness is. *What if bitterness is actually a seed of beautiful potential not yet planted in the rich soil of forgiveness?*

What if?

Pause and choose to sit with it all. The stinging pain of the loss. The sweetness of possibility. The guilt of how you may have weaponized your grief and hurt others. The forgiveness of a compassionate Savior. The honesty that resentment hasn't made anything better or more peaceful.

The consideration of how to let tenderness in again.

The thrill of more potential healing.

The deeper awareness that there's more beauty to see in this world, even in the midst of loss . . . or, better yet, especially because there is loss.

God, I know You are close to me when I'm experiencing loss. Help me process my grief in a healthy way, even in a way that releases bitterness from my heart. Show me where bitterness may be hiding out in me so I can truly move forward in the beauty of forgiveness and release the weight of my hurt and pain from my past. In Jesus' name, amen.

42

Healing Is Such a Process

Humble yourselves before the Lord, and he will lift you up.

James 4:10

One date night my husband, Art, and I bought a birthday card for a friend we hadn't seen or talked to in a long time.

Sending a card like this is good. It's saying, "I love you and I love that I have this marked moment, prompting me to celebrate you." But this card, this relationship was different.

It was a hard choice because this friend was no longer in my life. During a season when I needed them most, they'd been strangely absent. And they'd recruited others to be the same, which hurt even more.

So, in a deep-down place, I decided this person no longer got to hold space in my heart, in my calendar, or on my list of cards to be sent on holidays.

But there we were, making an exception. I was making space for them, and I wasn't entirely sure why.

Over our meal, we decided together what to write inside. And then at some point, Art sealed the envelope. I put a stamp on the outside, and I remember thinking, *Wow . . . look at me. I'm the bigger person here. I sure am doing well with all this healing stuff.*

We acknowledged once again that sending this card was the right thing to do. Then we drove to the post office and dropped the card off, and that was it.

Until an hour later, when I read an e-mail with some frustrating news that was totally unrelated to the person we'd sent the card to earlier. Someone hadn't properly done a job I had paid them to do, and now they were billing me for the extra time it would take to fix their mistake.

Normally this would have just prompted a simple phone call to the person and we'd have had a practical discussion around the issue. But instead, everything rational inside me felt paralyzed. I felt wronged. I felt taken advantage of and angry in a way that was way out of proportion to this situation. Thankfully, I didn't respond to the e-mail at that moment.

That feeling of "wrong" was like a magnet calling forth every other feeling of undealt-with wrongs. Though the person I'd sent the card to had nothing to do with the unexpected bill, the emotion I was feeling was connecting the two events as one.

And as much as I didn't want to admit it, bitterness was boiling up.

Bitterness isn't just a feeling. It is like liquid acid seeping into every part of us and corrupting all it touches. It not only reaches unhealed places, but it also eats away at all that is healed and healthy in us. Bitterness leaves nothing unaffected. Bitterness over one thing will locate bitterness hiding inside of us over other things. It will always intensify our reactions, skew our perspective, and take us further and further away from peace.

Bitterness . . . is like liquid acid seeping into every part of us and corrupting all it touches.

Instead of talking about fun and positive things on our date that night, I got very vocal about how frustrating it is when people are mean and hurtful.

Art listened to my venting. And then he calmly asked me, "Lysa, are you angry that you haven't seen evidence of God defending you?"

And there it was.

A moment of absolute clarity. Was this about God?

I hated that Art asked this question. And I loved that he asked the question.

I swallowed, hard. And answered him: "Yes, that's why I'm angry. I don't understand why God hasn't shown these people how wrong it was to do what they did and to feel convicted by all the devastation they caused."

Art then asked, "How do you know that He hasn't?"

Refusing to let my spiritual maturity perfect my answer, I

blurted out, "Because they haven't ever come back to me to acknowledge it or apologize."

Art calmly replied, "And maybe they never will. But that's not evidence against God. It's just where they are in the process."

The process. They have a process. But so do I. And I think it's time for me to make progress in my own process.

And as I've let it sit with me, I've realized there's something that needs to be added into my process: humility.

James 4:10 says, *"Humble yourselves before the Lord, and he will lift you up."*

Humanity rises up and demands that I be declared the right one. Humility bows low and realizes that only God has what I really want.

Turning my heart over to bitterness is me turning away from God. So I bow low, not because I want to. Because I need to. I prayed, "I release my need for this to feel fair. Show me what I need to learn."

Humility bows low and realizes that only God has what I really want.

Please understand, I am not saying feelings are wrong or bad. Not at all. But what we do with those feelings is the determining factor as to whether we will stay stuck in our pain or find healing perspectives. I know I'm stuck in pain when I get emotionally triggered at the mention of that person who was the source of the hurt.

I have a choice to keep adding my anger and resentment into the equation, or I can make the rare choice to add in my own humility. My anger and resentment demand that all the wrongs are made right. They also keep me positioned to get emotionally triggered over and over.

I know I'm healing when their name is mentioned and a life lesson is what I think about, and with a better perspective, I make better choices. It's all such a process . . . a process that has to start somewhere.

I knew we were supposed to send that birthday card. But when we placed it in the mailbox, my emotions had not yet voted yes. And that's okay.

Our emotions will sometimes be the very last thing to catch up to where we've healed. The card we sent felt like I was just going through the motions, but maybe it was walking out obedience.

This card was all part of the healing process.

I don't have to know if it will ever make a difference in that person's life. It made a difference in mine. It's part of my process of cooperating with God. And it is necessary. And it is good.

God, I give this situation to You. I release my need for an apology. I release my need for this to feel fair. I release my need for You to declare me right and them wrong. I want to embrace what You may be teaching me through this situation. Give me Your peace in place of my anger. In Jesus' name, amen.

A Letter from Lysa

Friend,

Never underestimate the beauty or the power of seemingly small moments. Little acts of kindness. Simple words of encouragement. Overlooking an offense. Letting someone else go first. Being patient with a child. Being generous with a neighbor.

When we get to heaven, I think we will be surprised by what actually mattered the most . . . what actually changed the world . . . what actually fulfilled the purpose for which we were created.

Look for opportunities to remind people of God's love in even the smallest of moments today.

Lysa

43

THE SLIPPERY SLOPE

To open their eyes and turn them from darkness to light, and from the power of Satan to God.

Acts 26:18

Friend, we've made a lot of progress together through these pages. As we move forward in healing from pain from the past, I think it's important for us to talk today about ways to protect ourselves from slipping back into old thoughts and patterns.

One of those dangerous patterns is justifying something we know isn't God's best.

If you've ever felt yourself being pulled into a forbidden but exciting situation, you may know exactly what I'm talking about. It's the script you can end up turning to when you sense red flags, but you want to convince yourself you can handle it. *I'm just having a little fun. This won't ever amount to anything. It just gives me a little something to look forward to.*

You brush off conviction.

You keep secrets from those people you know would lovingly hold you accountable.

You bend the truth.

You pretend.

And you forget what a voracious appetite sin has. Sin may seem like no big deal at first. But as apologist Ravi Zacharias said, "Sin will take you farther than you want to go, keep you longer than you want to stay, and cost you more than you want to pay."[4]

Yes, sin unleashes consequences that will rob us of our peace, diminish our integrity, and cause us pain that's never worth it.

That's exactly what happened to a friend of mine when a nice guy at work started paying attention to her. Her marriage was hard, and she was tired of trying. She found herself putting extra effort into getting dressed in the morning and being more than willing to work late.

Sin unleashes consequences that will rob us of our peace, diminish our integrity, and cause us pain that's never worth it.

She felt a spark in her heart every time he came near. Soon they were talking in secret. Texting in secret. Meeting in secret. And down the slippery slope she went.

The slippery slope has one major telltale sign: things are done in secret.

The minute we start hiding things from those who love us,

doing things in a sneaky way, lying or telling half-truths, and figuring out ways to cover up evidence of our activities—we're on the slippery slope. And we're headed downhill fast.

Satan is the master of darkness. As long as he can keep us operating in our dark secrets, we are deceived. As Eugene Peterson paraphrased Acts 26:17–18 in *The Message*:

> *I'm sending you off to open the eyes of the outsiders so they can see the difference between dark and light, and choose light, see the difference between Satan and God, and choose God. I'm sending you off to present my offer of sins forgiven, and a place in the family, inviting them into the company of those who begin real living by believing in me.*

Oh, dear friend, we need to see the difference between dark and light and choose light. We need to bring our choices out into the light of Jesus so He can expose the truth. Only then can we truly discern the difference between being led by Jesus and deceived by Satan. If we want to continue to move forward in healing, this is something we must not forget.

Doing things in secret can be an indication we are being led by Satan. That's a strong statement but one worth really considering.

Satan keeps dangers off our radar screen and blinds us to the harsh realities coming our way. My friend was blinded. And when she finally woke up to the deception, the devastation horrified her.

If you're keeping secrets today, I know it feels scary to bring what's really going on out into the light. But my friend would tell you, the darkness eventually turned on her. And what started out as fun soon became her worst nightmare. The only way out was to let trusted people in.

- Find a trusted Christian friend and ask them to help you hold your choices up to the truth.
- Get honest with people who love you.
- Admit you need help and take the time to get the help you need.
- Build accountability measures in your life.
- Ask Jesus for help, forgiveness, and a clear understanding of how to hit the brakes and throw things in reverse. Let His truth speak louder than the feelings that are begging you to keep things hidden. Like the end of verse 18 says, "Begin real living by believing in me."

The only regret you'll have after getting the help you need is that you didn't do it sooner. And please don't feel alone in that. There isn't one of us who hasn't needed to go through each of the steps I mentioned above.

The path to real living—the living that will sustain you and lead you to a true discovery of real love, real provision, and real satisfaction—is found only by following Jesus. Let's continue to walk this healing journey out together.

Dear Lord, help me bring any choices I'm making that don't line up with Your truth into the light. I pray that shame, guilt, and condemnation would have no grip on me. Thank You for Jesus . . . the only way that I can receive forgiveness of my sin. I receive the grace You have so graciously poured out for me. In Jesus' name, amen.

44

You Are Worth Celebrating

Charm is deceitful, and beauty is vain, but a woman who fears the Lord is to be praised.

Proverbs 31:30 ESV

Do you ever find yourself feeling like you don't measure up because of what you've been through?

Me too.

I remember when I first read Proverbs 31, which describes a woman of noble character, many years ago as a young wife and mom. I thought the Proverbs 31 woman was overwhelmingly perfect.

And as I've walked through hardship in my life over the last few years, I've found myself not just intimidated by Proverbs 31 but defeated by this wife whose marriage seemed full of praises. Even good marriages don't always have such shiny realities.

That's why my heart feels especially tender toward those of you who would rather skip over Proverbs 31. I know what it's like to have these words sit heavy on your heart with a resounding declaration of "I'm not enough."

But what if I told you the heart behind Proverbs 31:10–31 is one of celebration and not condemnation?

The first thing I want us to take note of is that this isn't just a chapter about a wife of noble character. It's a chapter about a woman of valor. A courageous woman. A woman of strength and dignity.

And the fact that you are reading this devotional, seeking God, and pursuing healing for the painful circumstances you've walked through is evidence that you are a woman of valor, courage, strength, and dignity. So Proverbs 31 is for you and me.

And in the Jewish culture, these verses are read out loud on the Sabbath as a celebration over the women. This is in no way condemning what they aren't, but celebrating how they, in their own unique expressions, live out the virtues detailed in this chapter. These aren't words meant to tell a woman she is supposed to be more. They are a celebration of who she is.

Isn't that the way it should be? Courageous women celebrating each other—and those they love celebrating them. All under the banner of honoring God, serving out of love, and smiling at the future.

These aren't words meant to tell a woman she is supposed to be more. They are a celebration of who she is.

I also love how Proverbs 31:30 reminds us of what is truly worth celebrating: *"Charm is deceitful, and beauty is vain, but a woman who fears the Lord is to be praised"* (ESV).

Notice it's not a woman with a spotless house who is to be praised. It's not the mom with perfectly behaved children who never skips pages when reading books to them. Honestly, it's not even just for a woman who is married and has children.

It's a woman who fears the Lord who is to be praised. This isn't an "I'm afraid of God" kind of fear. This type of fear is referring to having a heart completely in awe of God. It describes a woman who honors God by seeking Him in everything she does and trusting Him wholeheartedly with her life. She has a heart of reverence that overflows into a life of spiritual maturity and wisdom.

And let's not forget to look at today's verses within the context of why God gave us this book of the Bible. The very first chapter of Proverbs tells us it exists so we can gain wisdom, instruction, understanding, insight, knowledge, discretion, and guidance (vv. 1–7). Proverbs 2:1–5 goes on to remind us that as we receive and apply God's commands, we will be able to understand how to find the knowledge of the Lord.

Wisdom is both a gift from God and a process of learning.

I know this passage of Scripture can easily trip us up. But what if we take God at His Word and choose to believe these words hold good and pleasant things for us? What if we challenge ourselves to look at Proverbs 31 closely, seeing what part of it is a gift to us and what verses we need to learn from? What if we speak these words over ourselves and the other women in our lives as a form of celebration instead of condemnation, realizing that our stories don't disqualify us.

God tucked these words into His Word for all eternity, dear friend. And that tells me they are needed and meant for our good. Let's ask Him to help us learn from them today.

Father God, I confess that at times I look at the Proverbs 31 woman and feel like I will never be enough. But I realize the purpose isn't to shame me for all that I feel like I'm not. Her example is there to remind me to look to You and live for You in all that I do. Help me receive these words from You as a gift. And show me how to live them out according to the unique way You purposefully designed me. In Jesus' name, amen.

45

The Verses I Need Today

Come near to God and he will come near to you.

James 4:8

Sometimes we know things to be true with our heads, but when our hearts hurt and life gets really hard, we need reminders of God's presence, protection, and promise to help us. During the time that Art and I were separated, I experienced loneliness like I had never known. It was terrifying to wake up in the middle of the night when I heard something. It was painful to come home after work and eat dinner alone. And it was so hard facing each day not knowing if or when I'd ever feel normal again. I had to have something besides my ever-changing emotions to help guide me. I had to have a way to draw near to God and fight off the fear and the lies that kept attacking me. The most effective way I knew to draw near to God and be reminded He was with me was by getting into His Word and letting His truth become my daily declarations.

Declaring God's truth and lifting up our hearts in prayer is drawing near to God. James 4:8 says, *"Come near to God and he will come near to you."* So for those of you who, like me, could use an extra bit of help, I pulled some scriptures for us to declare over the parts of our lives that can be so vulnerable to attacks from the enemy.

Affection—my heart, what I love

"You will seek me and find me when you seek me with all your heart." (Jeremiah 29:13)

Now declare with me: "The Lord has promised me that when I seek Him with all my heart, I will find Him. He is not hiding from me or ignoring me. He is waiting to be seen by me. And so I am setting my heart's desire fully on Him today—declaring that He is the One I want above all else. Nothing and no one other than Him can ever fully satisfy my soul. My eyes are open, my ears are listening, and my heart is humbly expectant as I seek to truly know and experience my good and loving God."

Adoration—my mouth, what I worship

Ascribe to the Lord the glory due his name; worship the Lord in the splendor of his holiness. (Psalm 29:2)

Declare: "When difficult circumstances shout loud in my ear, I know exactly what I need to do. I need to get loud in return. Turning up my praise. Boldly declaring the truth of who my God is out loud for the enemy and my own shaky soul to hear. Because He is a God who deserves all glory and honor and praise. He is holy and wholly good. A promise-keeping God through and through. And no matter what my circumstances may say, He is forever worthy of my adoration and praise."

ATTENTION—MY MIND, WHAT I FOCUS ON

Since, then, you have been raised with Christ, set your hearts on things above, where Christ is, seated at the right hand of God. (Colossians 3:1)

Declare: "Sometimes my soul feels stuck in my circumstances, but I know this world is not my home. Its brokenness and hurt are not my destiny. And this pain and heartbreak will not be the end of my story. Today I'm purposefully choosing to lift my gaze. To set my heart and mind on the things above. I have the promise of eternity in heaven—a place where there will be no more tears and no more pain. And I have the sweet assurance of God's powerful presence

This pain and heartbreak will not be the end of my story.

and His perfect provision in the here and now. I am fixing my eyes on the hope He says is mine. The hope I have in Him."

Attraction—my eyes, what I desire

I will praise the Lord, who counsels me;
even at night my heart instructs me.
I keep my eyes always on the Lord.
With him at my right hand, I will not be shaken. (Psalm 16:7–8)

Declare: "It's so easy for my eyes to be attracted to things of this world to ease the aches of my disappointments. But anything that pulls my focus away from God's goodness isn't good for me. Therefore, I will keep my eyes on the Lord and trust Him to take my hand, steady my heart, and lead me to His best plans."

Ambition—my calling, what I spend my time seeking

Brothers and sisters, I do not consider myself yet to have taken hold of it. But one thing I do: Forgetting what is behind and straining toward what is ahead, I press on toward the goal to win the prize for which God has called me heavenward in Christ Jesus. (Philippians 3:13–14)

Declare: "There are so many moments when I forget what is ahead and dwell on what is already behind me. But when I fixate on my past, I place a stumbling block in the way of my future. I declare over my situation that I will look ahead toward the goal and prize of heaven that God has already promised to those who are His. And I am His. This is my future; this is my great ambition and joy. What has been left behind needs to stay behind; what is ahead needs to stay in the forefront of my thinking. I will press on, carry on, and lean on Him who has called me heavenward."

Action—my choices, how I stand firm

Put on the full armor of God, so that when the day of evil comes, you may be able to stand your ground, and after you have done everything, to stand. (Ephesians 6:13)

Declare: "Sometimes seasons of life leave me feeling weak and so weary. But I am reminding my soul today that I do not have to fight the enemy in my own strength. True and lasting strength comes from the Lord. The One who does battle with me and for me. The One who equips me to stand strong against the enemy. So today I lift my prayers and my praises up to Him as I clothe myself with His mighty armor. Yes, I'm fighting a battle of epic proportions. But I am fighting from victory, not for victory. In Christ, I've already won. And Satan is a defeated foe."

Dear God, I know lies must flee in the presence of truth. I want to fill up my heart and mind today with the truth of who You are. May Your Word simultaneously be the sword I use to fight my battles and the soothing love letter that settles my soul. I know that the enemy is a defeated foe, and I praise You for that victorious place I can live from today. In Jesus' name, amen.

46

The Best Thing You Can Do for Your Marriage Today

He [Jesus] also told them this parable: "Can the blind lead the blind? Will they not both fall into a pit?"

Luke 6:39

Recently I sat down to write some thoughts out to a young friend of mine getting married.

I wanted these words to be encouraging but also realistic. I didn't want to pen the typical "best wishes on your wedding day." Wishes might be sweet for a church full of flowers and white tulle, but it takes a whole lot more for a marriage to go the distance.

So I wrote honest thoughts as they came to me:

> Being married is amazing. Being married is challenging. Being married can seem impossibly hard. Being married can seem incredibly beautiful. There is no other person who can frustrate me the way my husband can. There is no other person who can make me feel as loved as my husband can.

As these words tumbled out, I wondered if my friend would think I was being a bit crazy. One minute I painted marriage as blissful as a kite catching wind and rising to the sky. And the next minute it was as if the string had gotten caught in a thorny bush and sent the kite crashing to the ground with a thud of disappointment.

So which is it? Bliss or disappointment? It's a fragile blend of both.

In the end, I crumpled up my original note and simply wrote this: "Determine to pray more words over your marriage than you speak about your marriage."

Many times when I've been going through a hard time, my friends have said, "Lysa, have you prayed about this?" I respond with total assurance, "Oh, absolutely I have prayed about it."

Determine to pray more words over your marriage than you speak about your marriage.

But the reality is, I've thought about it. Worried about it. Tried to control it. Manipulated it. Strategized around it. But I haven't really, really, really been down on my face before the Lord and said, "God, I don't like this. I really don't like this. It breaks my heart. Please help me."

Through everything Art and I have walked through, I can't think of a better piece of wisdom I could give to you than to pray for your marriage.

Art and I have committed to this. It gives us the freedom to just be with each other without the pressure of needing to fix each other. It's not that I don't bring up concerns, but I don't take Art's issues on as mine to fix. And Art doesn't take on mine either. We box out our frustrations in prayer with God or work on them with our counselors. It's not all tidy. It's actually sometimes quite messy—but it's good.

In Luke 6:39, Jesus asked an important but simple question: *"Can the blind lead the blind? Will they not both fall into a pit?"* My husband and I need Jesus leading us, guiding us, teaching us, redirecting us, and showing us how to have a marriage that honors Him and each other.

Praying more words over my marriage will certainly be key to this.

Today I want us to pray some scriptures specifically over our marriages together. And friend, if you are currently single and believing for marriage one day, use these scriptures to pray for your future husband. Or even pray for strengthened marriages represented in your community of friends. God has something for all of us today no matter what season we are in.

> *What, then, shall we say in response to these things? If God is for us, who can be against us?* (Romans 8:31)

We know and rely on the love God has for us. God is love. Whoever lives in love lives in God, and God in them. This is how love is made complete among us so that we will have confidence on the day of judgment: In this world we are like Jesus. There is no fear in love. But perfect love drives out fear, because fear has to do with punishment. The one who fears is not made perfect in love. We love because he first loved us. (1 John 4:16–19)

The LORD himself goes before you and will be with you; he will never leave you nor forsake you. Do not be afraid; do not be discouraged. (Deuteronomy 31:8)

By wisdom a house is built, and through understanding it is established; through knowledge its rooms are filled with rare and beautiful treasures. (Proverbs 24:3–4)

If you have any encouragement from being united with Christ, if any comfort from His love, if any common sharing in the Spirit, if any tenderness and compassion, then make my joy complete by being like-minded, having the same love, being one in spirit and of one mind. Do nothing out of selfish ambition or vain conceit. Rather, in humility value others above yourselves, not looking to your own interests but each of you to the interests of the others. (Philippians 2:1–4)

I'm convinced the more we battle out our struggles on our knees, the less we'll have to argue and fight about in person. And the freer we will be to simply focus on loving and living together, and that is beautiful.

Dear Lord, I want to honor You completely with my marriage. Help me remain dedicated to praying over my relationship with my husband. Help me see what You need me to see, learn what I need to learn, give what I need to give, and receive what I need to receive. Help me learn the rhythm of praying more words for my marriage than I speak about my marriage. In Jesus' name, amen.

A Letter from Lysa

Friend,

I'm not sure who else needs this assurance today, but I sure do:

We don't have to be fearful about what the future holds. God is already standing in every one of our tomorrows.

Standing there with His protection. Waiting on us with His wisdom. Going before us with His hope and His provision.

God is not shaken by what He sees in your tomorrow, and neither should you be. He is preparing you today with all that you'll need to handle . . . both the ups and downs that await you. Learn His lessons well today, and you'll be fully prepared for tomorrow.

There are good things ahead. Really good . . . because a really good God is there with His arms wide open with love.

Please don't forget this today.

Lysa

47

But How Do I Get Through the Next 86,400 Seconds?

The God of all grace, who called you to his eternal glory in Christ, after you have suffered a little while, will himself restore you and make you strong, firm and steadfast.

1 Peter 5:10

I want healing to be as neat and predictable as a checklist. I don't want to be inconvenienced by it, and I most certainly don't want to be caught off guard by the emotions that can go along with it.

Of course, if you've ever had to heal from having your heart broken in excruciating ways, you know you can't schedule healing. You can't hurry it up. And you can't control how and when it will want to be tended to.

Part of what makes healing so hard is the deep ache left behind after the trauma. Loss envelops us with an aching grief that comes in unpredictable waves. It's hard to know if you're getting better when a string of good days suddenly gives way to an unexpected emotional crash.

You feel angrier than ever over the unfairness of it all. The wounds seem raw, confusing, and unhealed. And you just wish someone would please tell you how in the world you're supposed to make it through all 86,400 seconds of this day in the midst of so much pain.

Trust me when I say I understand all of these feelings. When my marriage was in shambles, I remember wondering if my heart would ever feel whole again.

I believed God would make something new and wonderful from the dust of my circumstances, even if that didn't include restoring my marriage. I just didn't know how to function while hurting so much in the midst of daily life.

Like when I laid my head down on the banana display in the grocery store, completely spent. I was just standing there with an empty cart, a heart full of pain, and my face pressed into the display. The teenage worker saw me and couldn't figure out what I was doing. I guess he assumed my concern was about the choices of fruit before me. So, heaven help him, he asked, "Can I help you?" I turned my face toward him. Tears flooded out. And all I could think to say was, "I need a tissue."

Lovely. Nothing makes a day complete quite like a breakdown in front of an underpaid fruit attendant at the grocery store.

But I've discovered those days don't have to be setbacks. They can be evidence we're moving through the hardest parts of healing. The new tears over old wounds are proof we're tending to our emotions. We're processing the grief. We're wrestling well with the ache in our soul.

Feeling the pain is the first step toward healing the pain.

Feeling the pain is the first step toward healing the pain.

And all those emotions that keep bubbling up and unexpectedly spilling out? They're evidence you aren't dead inside. There's life under the surface. And while feelings shouldn't be dictators of how we live, they are great indicators of what still needs to be worked through.

When we love deeply, we hurt deeply. This is why we have to learn how to trust the process of healing. We have to let it ebb and flow around, in, and through us. We have to grant it access to our heart.

And when we start to see healing as unfolding layers of unexpected strength and richly revealed wisdom, it doesn't feel so unfair. It starts to feel like the sweetest secret God ever whispered into the depth of our soul.

Then one day we suddenly realize the future feels stunningly appealing. Not because circumstances have changed but because we have embraced reality, released control, and found this healed version of ourselves is what we'd been looking for all along.

I don't know what kind of pain or heartbreak you may be walking through right now. But I do want to point you toward the hope found in our key verse: *"The God of all grace, who called you to his eternal glory in Christ, after you have suffered a little while, will himself restore you and make you strong, firm and steadfast"* (1 Peter 5:10).

Our God is a God of restoration. And all that aching within you is proof there's a beautiful remaking in process. Don't give up.

God loves you. You are not alone. Healing *is* possible.

Father God, when all I want is to be done with my healing journey, remind me that I can trust You in this process. Thank You for being a God who keeps His promises. I know You will use this heartbreak for good. In Jesus' name, amen.

48

I Still Get Scared Sometimes

He who dwells in the shelter of the Most High
will abide in the shadow of the Almighty.
I will say to the Lord, "My refuge and my
fortress, my God, in whom I trust."

Psalm 91:1–2 ESV

I leaned over to Art and confessed, "I still get scared sometimes."

He patiently replied, "Of course you do. Do you want to talk about it or just sit here together?"

Like you and I talked about in our reading yesterday, we have to trust the process of our healing. Through my process, fear has been a challenging chapter of my healing to tackle. When I've been hurt, I get afraid.

It's not lost on me that some of man's first recorded words to God after eating the forbidden fruit were, *"I was afraid because I was naked; so I hid"* (Genesis 3:10).

I relate to those words on deep levels. I am afraid to be emotionally naked . . . exposed . . . unsure . . . uncertain if I will get hurt again. Those "what if" questions nip at the most tender places of my heart, and I wonder if I will be devoured if any of them become devastatingly true.

That fear of the future is what makes me whisper to Art, "I still get afraid sometimes." Life doesn't come with any guarantees that we won't hurt again. Even Jesus Himself reminded us, *"I have told you these things, so that in me you may have peace. In this world you will have trouble. But take heart! I have overcome the world"* (John 16:33). When you've experienced deep hurt, you very much understand the trouble Jesus referenced. And you very much need to know that Jesus has overcome the world. But how do we see that in practical ways right now, in this moment, in this situation?

I love that today's key verses found in Psalm 91 give us a script to say to ourselves in moments we get afraid and triggered: *"I will say to the LORD, 'My refuge and my fortress, my God, in whom I trust.'"*

Isn't it interesting that the psalmist described God here as a refuge and a fortress?

A refuge is a quick place you duck into to find shelter. A fortress is a place built intentionally for the purposes of exceptional security. The Hebrew word for fortress is *metsudah*, with one of its definitions being an "inaccessible place."

God is not just a quick refuge from the storms of life; He's also the place where fear no longer has access to me. Fear can't catch what it can no longer reach.

God is not just a quick refuge from the storms of life; He's also the place where fear no longer has access to me.

To experience this level of peace, we must be near to God. It is a nearness we see described throughout Psalm 91 as we are reminded to *"abide in the shadow of the Almighty"* (v. 1 ESV), take refuge under His wings, (v. 4), and make Him our dwelling place (v. 9).

Just as we must sit close enough to a tree to enjoy the benefits of its shade from the sun's scorching heat, so we must also position ourselves near to God if we desire His comfort, protection, and deliverance.

It's not that bad things won't ever happen to us. Life is rarely tidy. Relationships aren't easy. And the constant stresses and strains of managing and navigating so many daily issues are hard on the human heart. I can find myself feeling one minute like I'm doing really well with keeping my heart swept clean of bitterness and the next minute feeling like a complete failure. Old triggers beg us to give into fear of what could be around the next corner.

But as a child of God, I know I'm not supposed to live with fear taunting and terrorizing me.

And as I've sat with these feelings, I've come to the conclusion that the goal of having the peace Jesus referred to in John 16:33 isn't perfection; it's progress.

I'm learning to make progress with my fear. I now know I can feel afraid, but I don't have to live afraid of the future. I can be present in this day without letting fear of tomorrow steal my peace today. I can only attend to what is right in front of me. I must trust God to hold the future.

The sign of progress is to let the fear drive you to remember God and run to Him instead of forgetting Him and letting fear run rampant in your heart and mind.

I can feel afraid, but I don't have to live afraid of the future.

When fear comes, use it as an opportunity to form the new healing habits and perspectives we've been discovering together in this journey.

- Have one better thought.
- Have one better reaction.
- Have one better way to process.
- Have one better conversation.
- Have one better boundary you lovingly communicate and consistently keep.
- Have one better choice to not reach for that substance to numb out.

- Have one better heart-pivot toward forgiveness instead of resentment.
- Have one better situation where you make fear bow to your trust in God.
- Have one less day where you stay afraid or mad or frustrated.
- Have one less hour when you refuse grace.

I look back at Art and take his hand. I realize we haven't done this journey perfectly. But as we step forward, I realize imperfect progress is good. So very good.

Lord, thank You that You sent Jesus, who deeply understands how hard it can be to process fear inside these frail, hurting human hearts of ours. Thank You for the hope that Jesus has overcome the world. Now help me overcome what I'm facing today. Thank You for the grace that I don't have to do it perfectly. I just have to make progress. I love You, Lord. In Jesus' name, amen.

49

Delicate, Not Fragile

You, Lord, are our Father. We are the clay, you are the potter; we are all the work of your hand.

Isaiah 64:8

When I was walking through one of the most difficult seasons of my life, God showed me a powerful picture. I'm not really a "see some sort of vision" kind of girl. So at first I thought it was just my imagination wandering off for a minute. But then I felt an impression on my heart that this wasn't random; this really was from God.

At first, what I saw inside my mind was a beautiful flower made from paper-thin glass. I looked at it from all sides and admired the way it was formed. Then I saw a hand reaching out and wrapping itself around the glass flower. But as the hand closed around it, the glass popped and shattered. The glass was delicately beautiful but too fragile to be worked with.

Next, I saw the same flower formed out of shiny metal. And the hand reached out and wrapped itself around the flower and held it for a few seconds. But then once again the hand closed around it. Only this time nothing happened to the flower. It didn't change in any way. And I could tell the harder the hand pressed, the more pain the steel flower was causing the hand. The steel was strong but not moldable. The metal flower was too hard to give way to the hand's desired working.

But the last time I saw the same flower, it was made from a white clay. Every detail was the same except now when the hand reached out and closed around it, the flower moved with the hand. The clay squeezed and moved between the hand's fingers. The hand folded and twisted and worked with the clay until suddenly an even more beautiful flower emerged.

So I asked God about the glass flower and the metal flower. They were beautiful, but not as beautiful as the white clay flower after being molded.

I felt the Lord say to my heart, *Lysa, I want you to be delicate, but I don't want you to be fragile. If you're like that piece of glass, beautiful but so fragile, when I press into you and try to make you something new, you'll just shatter. I also want you to be strong, but I don't want you to be unmoldable. You see, Lysa, that steel flower, it'll always just be a steel flower. And no matter how hard My hand presses on it I can't make something new from something so hard. You are already beautiful, but if you'll surrender to My shaping, I can do a new and beautiful work in you.*

The images I had seen were beginning to make sense. He wanted me to be like clay. The white clay flower was delicately beautiful but not too fragile. The white clay flower was strong enough to hold its shape but soft enough to allow the hand to reshape me as needed. And in the end, the clay flower wound up being the most beautifully shaped of them all.

I felt the Lord say to my heart, Lysa, I want you to be delicate, but I don't want you to be fragile.

I cried. I finally felt like I could understand a bit of God's perspective.

It gave a whole new meaning to one of my favorite verses found in Isaiah 64:8: *"You, LORD, are our Father. We are the clay, you are the potter; we are all the work of your hand."*

Oh, friend, God isn't ever going to forsake us, but He will go to great lengths to remake us.

God loves the parts of us that are delicately beautiful, but He doesn't want us to be fragile like that glass. God made us to be strong, but He doesn't want us to grow hard like metal and unable to be molded.

Seeing beautiful again requires us to stay moldable by God. We don't want to be too fragile or too rigid. If we're too fragile, the fear of being broken, crushed, and hurt again will make us want to fight the process. If we are too rigid, those sharp and strong edges may feel like they protect us, but in reality, they just prevent the transformative work of God in us. It's only in

God isn't ever going to forsake us, but He will go to great lengths to remake us.

trusting the gentle but powerful hands of the Potter and allowing Him to remold and remake us that those hurts are able to be shaped into something beautiful.

He wants me like the clay, able to stand firm but still be molded and reformed into whatever purpose He has for me. He wants that for you too, my friend. We don't have to be afraid of how He's going to shape our lives. He is the God who makes everything beautiful in its time.

God, help me turn my eyes away from my circumstances and to trusting You as the Potter, making something beautiful out of it all. I want to be moldable so I can become more like You. Remind me of the illustration of these different flowers often. In Jesus' name, amen.

50

Living Beautiful

"That they may be brought to complete unity. Then the world will know that you sent me and have loved them even as you have loved me."

John 17:23

Friend, I'm so glad we've had this time together.

We got honest. We processed. We prayed. We dared to hope again. Love again. Be compassionate again. Tenderhearted again. Then we realized together that forgiveness is a gift from God meant to be opened every day. And finally we got to the place where we realize seeing beautiful again has a lot less to do with the circumstances right in front of us and a lot more to do with using God's truth to frame our perspective.

So as we arrive at the final day in our journey together, I want us to look at the last words Jesus shared with us.

Even though I treasure reading about the last moments of Jesus' life with His friends, at the same time, my heart aches. He knew all that was about to happen to Him. Within hours of this last time together, He knew:

One of them would betray Him.

The others would not stand with Him.

He would soon endure extreme brutality all alone.

And yet, somehow, He was focused enough to stay very present in this moment instead of living in dread of the horrific moments to come.

It astounds me how present and giving Jesus was during the Last Supper. Jesus and the disciples ate together. They drank together. They talked. He washed their feet. He watched Judas walk out the door.

Then He prayed. For Himself. For the disciples.

And then for you and for me.

The fact that Jesus thought of and prayed for us in these final hours also astounds me.

I need to read what He prayed. But even more important, I need to live what He prayed.

> *"That they may be brought to complete unity. Then the world will know that you sent me and have loved them even as you have loved me."* (John 17:23)

Unity. Love.

Of all the many things He could have prayed for us, it was unity and love.

This feels a bit complicated in our world that seems so very divided on issues where so many have loud opinions, express strong objections, and feel very justified getting offended by almost anything.

I get it.

There's a lot of wrong in this world that should be addressed. There are a lot of injustices that should be defended. And there's a lot of evil that should be stopped.

But when I sit back quietly and observe, I wonder if there's a more unified way we are supposed to be doing this. We have an enemy, but it's not each other. In light of Jesus' last prayer for us before the cross, I wonder if we all need to remember that while we can be divided in our opinions, we can be a little more united in our compassion for one another.

After all, so much of what shapes the opinions and objections we express comes from some deep pain we've been through or walked through with someone we love. Hurt shapes us for better or worse. Jesus knew this. And He knew humans have such a propensity to turn hurting into hating. Maybe that's why He prayed for unity. Maybe it's not the kind of unity where we all agree but rather in the middle of disagreements, we would care to remember we are all carriers of pain and sorrow. Even if we don't see eye to eye, surely we could remember that we are so very alike in what makes us cry.

Hurt shapes us for better or worse. Jesus knew this.

Even if we are completely divided on everything else, we could remember that we're so very united in our tears and in our love for Jesus. And in that shared commonality we show the world that with Jesus, unity and peace are possible.

And where there is that kind of unity between us, the world looks a lot more beautiful around us.

This is seeing beautiful again. It's acknowledging what is. It's accepting what isn't. It's offering to use what you learned through your hurt to ease someone else's pain. It's believing that Jesus didn't utter that prayer of unity in vain. It's determining to look a little more like our Creator by taking what's in front of us and creating something beautiful from it—whether that's with a paintbrush, shattered pottery, or a changed perspective. It's declaring, even in the darkest night, that one light matters. It's remembering even a flicker of compassion, forgiveness, kindness, grace, and hope casts the most gorgeous light where we can be drawn together.

Where there is unity between us, the world looks a lot more beautiful around us.

Then the world will know
by our unity
and by our love
that Jesus was sent by God to redeem the world.

And because of Him, it is possible to not just see beautiful but live beautiful.

Father God, You long for me to receive the love of Jesus and to live it out. For me to walk in unity and in love. Help me tear down the barriers of judgment and hatred. Help me hold to Your Truth and walk in Your grace while sincerely loving others. Help me use my healing as a way to connect with others, human to human, no matter where I may be on my journey. May my heart be softened and my life be changed by Your call to unity and love. Help me to not just see beautiful but to live beautiful. In Jesus' name, amen.

Notes

1. Seth Stephens-Davidowitz, "Googling for God," *New York Times*, 2015, https://www.nytimes.com/2015/09/20/opinion/sunday/seth-stephens-davidowitz-googling-for-god.html.
2. "The basic feature of the Greek concept of εἰρήνη is that the word does not primarily denote a relationship between several people, or an attitude, but a state, i.e., 'time of peace' or 'state of peace,' originally conceived of purely as an interlude in the everlasting state of war." Werner Foerster, "Εἰρήνη, Εἰρηνεύω, Εἰρηνικός, Εἰρηνοποιός, Εἰρηνοποιέω," ed. Gerhard Kittel, Geoffrey W. Bromiley, and Gerhard Friedrich, *Theological Dictionary of the New Testament* (Grand Rapids, MI: Eerdmans, 1964), 400.
3. Taken from *Encouragement for Today: Devotions for Everyday Living* by Renee Swope, Lysa TerKeurst, Samantha Reed, and the Proverbs 31 Team, © 2013 by Proverbs 31 Ministry. Used by permission of Zondervan. www.zondervan.com.
4. GoodReads.com, https://www.goodreads.com/quotes/746709-sin-will-take-you-farther-than-you-want-to-go.

A Prayer from Lysa

If you declare with your mouth, "Jesus is Lord," and believe in your heart that God raised him from the dead, you will be saved.

Romans 10:9

When I was in my early twenties, I felt very distant from God. A series of heartbreaking situations in my life made me question His goodness and whether or not He really loved me. But through His divine grace, eventually truth broke through my cold resistance and brought me to the place where I wanted to accept His love and dedicate my life to Him.

The challenge was that I didn't know how to do this and I was too afraid to ask my friends. As I remembered struggling through this years ago, I wondered if you might be facing this same struggle too. Maybe you've had some ups and downs with this whole God thing but finally you're in a place where you want to give your heart to Him, accept His grace, and receive salvation.

If that's you, I'd like to invite you to pray this salvation prayer with me today:

A Prayer from Lysa

Dear God,

Thank You for the gifts of grace and forgiveness. Thank You that in the midst of my sin, You have made a way, through Jesus, to forgive my sin and make me right with You.

So today I confess my sinfulness . . . my hard heart . . . my mean thoughts . . . my harsh words . . . my doubt. I believe with all my heart that it was for me—and because of me—that Jesus died.

Please forgive me of all my sin. Big sins. Small sins. Past sins. Present sins. And all sins to come. I exchange my sin for Jesus' goodness and holiness. By the shed blood of Jesus, I am now forgiven and free! Thank You that in this moment, You have sealed me with Your Holy Spirit. I receive this precious gift and trust You will do as You promise and make me a new creation, molding and shaping me from the inside out to be more like You!

I celebrate that the old me is gone and the new me is here to stay! I love You and am forever grateful for Your forgiveness and my new life in You. I ask all this in Jesus' name. Amen.

I love you, dear friend. And I'm rejoicing with all of heaven over every decision made to accept God's free gift of salvation. It truly is the sweetest gift we'll ever receive.

Beautiful Truths to Remember: Twenty Scriptures to Hold onto When You're Still Hurting

Hi friend,

I deeply understand that when unexpected hurt shatters the way we thought our lives would be today, we can easily start to become guarded with others and skeptical of God.

But can I share something I've been learning with you?

Right now—in the middle of what's breaking your heart—that aching pain you feel is actually proof there's a beautiful remaking in process.

You see, seeing beautiful again is not just a good idea or a special opportunity for someone else with different circumstances than yours. It's not even about mustering up enough courage to make something better or overriding your feelings to pretend you're fine when you're crying yourself to sleep at night.

It's about opening your eyes to the breathtaking goodness already in front of you. It is a hopeful perspective for you to walk in right now.

It is a hopeful perspective for you to walk in right now as you declare that because of Jesus, you are more than what has happened to you, been taken from you, and what can never be the same.

We can't change what happened to us. But we get to choose how we move forward even if we're still hurting.

I want this truth to illustrate all the beautiful possibilities ahead, instead of carrying the heaviness of the past into the days to come.

I want this for you, too, friend.

So my prayer is that the truth tucked inside these scriptures will help carry you through whatever you're currently facing and help you remember this: Your life can still be beautiful.

Don't forget these words.

Love,

"He gives strength to the weary
and increases the power of the weak."

Isaiah 40:29 NIV

"He is the Maker of heaven and earth,
the sea, and everything in them—
he remains faithful forever."

Psalm 146:6 NIV

"So do not fear, for I am with you;
do not be dismayed, for I am your God.
I will strengthen you and help you;
I will uphold you with my righteous right hand."

ISAIAH 41:10 NIV

"You are my hiding place;
you will protect me from trouble
and surround me with songs of deliverance."

PSALM 32:7 NIV

"Consider it pure joy, my brothers and sisters, whenever
you face trials of many kinds, because you know
that the testing of your faith produces perseverance.
Let perseverance finish its work so that you may be
mature and complete, not lacking anything."

JAMES 1:2-4 NIV

"Let us hold unswervingly to the hope we
profess, for he who promised is faithful."

HEBREWS 10:23 NIV

"The Lord
is near."

Philippians 4:5 niv

"The Lord is near to
all who call on him,
to all who call on
him in truth."

Psalm 145:18 niv

"You intended to harm me, but God
intended it for good to accomplish what is
now being done, the saving of many lives."

Genesis 50:20 niv

"The Lord your God is with you,
the Mighty Warrior who saves.
He will take great delight in you;
in his love he will no longer rebuke you,
but will rejoice over you with singing.'"

Zephaniah 3:17 niv

"Let the peace of Christ rule in your hearts, since as
members of one body you were called to peace."

Colossians 3:15 niv

"The Lord has heard
my cry for mercy;
the Lord accepts
my prayer."

PSALM 6:9 NIV

"So we fix our eyes not
on what is seen, but on
what is unseen, since what
is seen is temporary, but
what is unseen is eternal."

2 CORINTHIANS 4:18 NIV

"Yet this I call to mind
and therefore I have hope:
Because of the Lord's great love we are not consumed,
for his compassions never fail.
They are new every morning;
great is your faithfulness."

LAMENTATIONS 3:21-23 NIV

"Be joyful in hope, patient in affliction, faithful
in prayer. Share with the Lord's people who
are in need. Practice hospitality."

ROMANS 12:12-13 NIV

"I will praise the Lord, who counsels me;
even at night my heart instructs me.
I keep my eyes always on the Lord.
With him at my right hand, I will not be shaken."

Psalm 16:7-8 NIV

"Brothers and sisters, I do not consider myself yet to have taken hold of it. But one thing I do: Forgetting what is behind and straining toward what is ahead, I press on toward the goal to win the prize for which God has called me heavenward in Christ Jesus."

Philippians 3:13-14 NIV

"But you, Lord, are a
shield around me,
my glory, the One who
lifts my head high."

Psalm 3:3 NIV

"'Blessed are the
poor in spirit,
for theirs is the
kingdom of heaven.
Blessed are those who mourn,
for they will be comforted.'"

Matthew 5:3-4 NIV

"In all this you greatly rejoice, though now for a little while you may have had to suffer grief in all kinds of trials. These have come so that the proven genuineness of your faith—of greater worth than gold, which perishes even though refined by fire—may result in praise, glory and honor when Jesus Christ is revealed."

1 Peter 1:6-7 niv

(For a printed version of this free resource, visit https://proverbs31.org/beautifultruth)

About the Author

Photograph by Kelsie Gorham

Lysa TerKeurst is the president of Proverbs 31 Ministries and the #1 *New York Times* bestselling author of *Forgiving What You Can't Forget, It's Not Supposed to Be This Way, Uninvited, The Best Yes*, and more than twenty other books. But to those who know her best she's just a simple girl with a well-worn Bible who proclaims hope in the midst of good times and heartbreaking realities.

Lysa lives with her family in Charlotte, North Carolina. Connect with her on a daily basis, see pictures of her family, and follow her speaking schedule:

Website: www.LysaTerKeurst.com

Click on "events," then "speaking & booking" to inquire about having Lysa speak at your event.

Facebook: www.Facebook.com/OfficialLysa

Instagram: @LysaTerKeurst

Twitter: @LysaTerKeurst

If you enjoyed *Seeing Beautiful Again*, equip yourself with additional resources at www.ForgivingWhatYouCantForget.com, www.LysaTerKeurst.com, and www.Proverbs31.org.

ABOUT PROVERBS 31 MINISTRIES

Lysa TerKeurst is the president of Proverbs 31 Ministries, located in Charlotte, North Carolina.

If you were inspired by *Seeing Beautiful Again* and desire to deepen your own personal relationship with Jesus Christ, we have just what you're looking for.

Proverbs 31 Ministries exists to be a trusted friend who will take you by the hand and walk by your side, leading you one step closer to the heart of God through:

Free *First 5* Bible study app
Free online daily devotions
Online Bible studies
Podcasts (You might find Lysa's Therapy and Theology series very helpful as you continue your pursuit of staying spiritually and emotionally healthy.)
COMPEL Writer Training
She Speaks Conference
Books and resources

Our desire is to help you to know the Truth and live the Truth. Because when you do, it changes everything.

For more information about Proverbs 31 Ministries, visit

www.Proverbs31.org.

To inquire about having Lysa speak at your event, visit

www.LysaTerKeurst.com and click on "events".

© Justin Smith with Vinyet Architecture

When my family and I were trying to heal from the darkest season of our lives, I kept praying that we'd one day be able to use our experiences to help others find healing. But I didn't just want to do this at conferences. I've dreamed of inviting friends like you over to my home to break bread and share our broken hearts, face to face, heart to heart. So, I'd love to invite you to Haven Place—a safe space for you to find the biblical and emotional healing you've been looking for.

If you'd like more information on the intimate gatherings, Bible studies, and retreats we'll be having here, such as:

- You, Me & We: Stop Dancing with Dysfunction in Your Relationships
- Forgiving What You Can't Forget
- Moving On When Your Marriage Doesn't
- Healing When You're Still Hurting

. . . please visit lysaterkeurst.com/invitation-from-lysa.

I truly believe healing, hope, and forgiveness will be the anthem songs, prayers, and shouts of victory that will rise from this Haven Place.

Also Available from Lysa TerKeurst

Forgiving What You Can't Forget: Discover How to Move On, Make Peace with Painful Memories, and Create a Life That's Beautiful Again

The Forgiveness Journal: A Guided Journey to Forgiving What You Can't Forget

Trustworthy: Overcoming Our Greatest Struggles to Trust God

It's Not Supposed to Be This Way: Finding Unexpected Strength When Disappointments Leave You Shattered

Embraced: 100 Devotions to Know God Is Holding You Close

Uninvited: Living Loved When You Feel Less Than, Left Out, and Lonely

The Best Yes: Making Wise Decisions in the Midst of Endless Demands

Finding I AM: How Jesus Fully Satisfies the Cry of Your Heart

Unglued: Making Wise Choices in the Midst of Raw Emotions

Made to Crave: Satisfying Your Deepest Desire with God, Not Food

Index by Topic

Anxiety/Fear, 91, 168, 242
Boundaries, 81, 87, 193, 210
Celebration, 32, 172, 222
Conflict, 45, 87
Conversations, 45, 105
Disappointment, 13, 27, 36, 63, 91, 110, 139, 154
Forgiveness, 96, 100, 128, 159, 164, 178, 184, 189, 205, 217, 242
God's Love, 59, 77, 110, 144, 159, 172, 189, 226, 238, 247, 251
God's Plan, 13, 22, 32, 36, 40, 68, 114, 124, 139, 168
Grief, 105, 144, 159, 205
Healing, 59, 72, 128, 133, 172, 205, 210, 217, 226, 238, 247, 251
Hope, 114, 124
Marriage, 87, 133, 178, 189, 193, 232,
Negative Thoughts, 17, 27, 63, 119, 139, 144, 210
Peace, 17, 164, 251
Perseverance, 22, 55, 68, 72, 110, 119, 154, 238, 247, 251
Prayer, 68, 124, 144, 154, 184, 193, 200, 232
Rejection, 50, 59
Relationships, 17, 45, 50, 81, 87, 96, 100, 105, 128, 133, 159, 164, 178, 189, 193, 200, 205, 217, 232, 242
Replacing Lies, 27, 63, 119, 144, 159, 226
Resentment, 50, 178, 184, 205, 210, 217
Surrender, 149
Time with God, 77
Trust, 13, 22, 36, 40, 55, 72, 81, 91, 114, 149, 168, 222
Wisdom, 77, 149, 164, 200, 222, 232, 251

Index by Devotion

The Process Before the Promise—Disappointment, Trust, God's Plan, 13

The Best Place to Park Your Mind Today—Peace, Negative Thoughts, Relationships, 17

I Don't Want This to Be Part of My Story—Perseverance, Trust, God's Plan, 22

Is This News or Truth?—Negative Thoughts, Replacing Lies, Disappointment, 27

When Joy Feels So Very Unrealistic—Joy, Celebration, God's Plan, 32

Why Would You Let This Happen, God?—Expectations, Trust, God's Plan, 36

Step After Step of Unwavering Obedience—Obedience, Trust, God's Plan, 40

Three Questions to Ask Before Giving a Response You Can't Take Back—Relationships, Conversations, Conflict, 45

Is It Really That Big of a Deal If I Stay Offended?—Relationships, Rejection, Resentment, 50

This Won't Be For Nothing—Purpose, Trust, Perseverance, 55

The Only Love that Never Fails—God's Love, Healing, Rejection, 59

When I Deny Jesus—Disappointment, Negative Thoughts, Replacing Lies, 63

Three Perspectives to Remember When Your Normal Gets Hijacked—Perseverance, God's Plan, Prayer, 68

Saved by Suffering—Healing, Trust, Perseverance, 72

Sometimes It's a One- or Two-Verse Day—Time with God, Wisdom, God's Love, 77

When Things Get Worse Just Before They Get Better—Trust, Relationships, Boundaries, 81

The Blessing of Boundaries—Boundaries, Relationships, Conflict, Marriage, 87

Where Is My Happily Ever After?—Trust, Disappointment, Anxiety/Fear, 91

When Giving Grace Feels Hard—Relationships, God's Grace, Forgiveness, 96

Forgiveness: The Double-Edged Word—Forgiveness, God's Grace, Relationships, 100

Please Don't Give Me a Christian Answer—Grief, Relationships, Conversations, Reactions, 105

When God Gives You More Than You Can Handle—God's Love, Perseverance, Disappointment, 110

Index by Devotion

An Unexpected Thread of Hope—Hope, God's Plan, Trust, 114

A Script to Preach to Myself—Replacing Lies, Negative Thoughts, Perseverance, 119

Higher Perspective in Present Realities—God's Plan, Hope, Prayer, 124

A New Way to Walk and a New Way to See—Healing, Forgiveness, Relationships, 128

When the Only Thing You Have Left to Give Is Time—Marriage, Relationships, Healing, Reconciliation, 133

God's Goodness Isn't Canceled—Disappointment, God's Plan, Negative Thoughts, 139

Why Isn't God Answering My Prayer?—Prayer, Grief, Negative Thoughts, Replacing Lies, God's Love, 144

When Our Opinions and Feelings Get Us In Trouble—Surrender, Trust, Wisdom, 149

The One We Really Need Today—Prayer, Disappointment, Perseverance, 154

When Unchangeable Feels Unforgivable—Grief, Forgiveness, Relationships, God's Love, Replacing Lies, 159

As Far As It Depends on Me—Peace, Relationships, Forgiveness, Wisdom, 164

Suspicious of God—Trust, God's Plan, Anxiety/Fear, 168

Brushstrokes of Compassion—Healing, Celebration, God's Love, 172

About My Anger—Forgiveness, Relationships, Marriage, Resentment, God's Grace, 178

The Daily Cure for a Heavy Heart—Prayer, Forgiveness, God's Grace, Resentment, 184

More Than Dust and Bone—Relationships, Marriage, Forgiveness, God's Love, 189

When Your Husband Has Given Up—Relationships, Marriage, Boundaries, Prayer, 193

Five Things to Say to a Friend Today—Relationships, Prayer, Wisdom, 200

Let Bitterness Be a Seed of Potential, Not a Root of Regret—Resentment, Forgiveness, Healing, Relationships, Grief, 205

Healing Is Such a Process—Healing, Resentment, Boundaries, Negative Thoughts, 210

The Slippery Slope—Resentment, Healing, Relationships, Forgiveness, 217

You Are Worth Celebrating—Celebration, Joy, Trust, Wisdom

The Verses I Need Today—Replacing Lies, Healing, God's Love, 222

The Best Thing You Can Do for Your Marriage Today—Marriage, Prayer, Wisdom, Relationships, 232

But How Do I Get Through the Next 86,400 Seconds?—Healing, Perseverance, God's Love, 238

Index by Devotion

I Still Get Scared Sometimes—Anxiety/Fear, Relationships, Forgiveness, 242

Delicate, Not Fragile—Healing, Perseverance, God's Love, 247

Living Beautiful—God's Love, Perseverance, Healing, Peace, Wisdom, 251

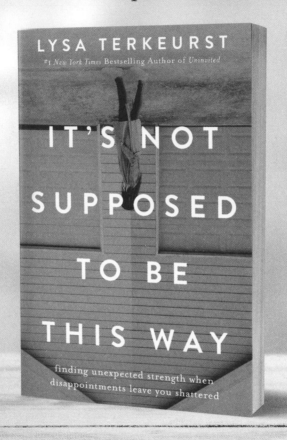

JOURNAL

Journal

Journal

JOURNAL

JOURNAL

Journal

Journal

Journal

JOURNAL

Journal

Journal

Journal